T0149474

You Are the Beauty

Art as a Path to Self-Discovery

AZITA TABIB

Copyright © 2018 Azita Tabib.

All rights reserved. No part of this book may be used or reproduced by any means, graphic, electronic, or mechanical, including photocopying, recording, taping or by any information storage retrieval system without the written permission of the author except in the case of brief quotations embodied in critical articles and reviews.

Balboa Press books may be ordered through booksellers or by contacting:

Balboa Press
A Division of Hay House
1663 Liberty Drive
Bloomington, IN 47403
www.balboapress.com
1 (877) 407-4847

Because of the dynamic nature of the Internet, any web addresses or links contained in this book may have changed since publication and may no longer be valid. The views expressed in this work are solely those of the author and do not necessarily reflect the views of the publisher, and the publisher hereby disclaims any responsibility for them.

The author of this book does not dispense medical advice or prescribe the use of any technique as a form of treatment for physical, emotional, or medical problems without the advice of a physician, either directly or indirectly. The intent of the author is only to offer information of a general nature to help you in your quest for emotional and spiritual well-being. In the event you use any of the information in this book for yourself, which is your constitutional right, the author and the publisher assume no responsibility for your actions.

Print information available on the last page.

Publisher's Cataloging-In-Publication Data
(Prepared by The Donohue Group, Inc.)

Names: Tabib, Azita.
Title: You are the beauty : art as a path to self-discovery / Azita Tabib.
Description: Bloomington, IN : Balboa Press, a division of Hay House, [2018]
Identifiers: ISBN 9781504389914 (softcover) | ISBN 9781504389938 (hardcover) | ISBN 9781504389921 (ebook)
Subjects: LCSH: Art--Philosophy. | Aesthetics. | Self-actualization (Psychology) | Beauty, Personal.
Classification: LCC N71 .T33 2018 (print) | LCC N71 (ebook) | DDC 701.15--dc23

Library of Congress Control Number: 2017915948

Balboa Press rev. date: 02/13/2018

To

All the lines,

And all the colors,

And to all blank pages in the world

That are waiting

For a day

When a hand

Sets them free

From an undefined destiny.

Azita, 1988

Many thanks to my great teacher Maya Machawe, yoga master and co-founder of Cyclic Yoga, whose inspiring teachings shed light on my way. Many thanks to Dr. Wayne Dyer, renowned author whose words in a coincidental conversation encouraged me to publish this book. Many thanks to Pam Barr for her all time support and her deep insight. And gratitude for my daughters who always encouraged me along the way, and helped me with their knowledge and support.

Contents

Preface

The dedication page you saw in the beginning of this book is a dedication page I wrote in 1988 for my thesis on Treatment of Chondromalacia Patellae, a common reason for knee pain in young adults, before I graduate with a B.S. degree in Physical Therapy. It seemed very odd at the time, since it was irrelevant to what's expected from a physical therapist's ambition, but it was truly meaningful to me.

As long as I remember, I had this longing to dedicate my time and abilities to an indescribable essence of life energy through art. The more I learned about human anatomy, bio mechanics, psychology, etc., the more I found myself drawing and painting human portraits and figures. Medical illustrations, portraits of roommates and friends from the dorm, drawing portraits of bored patients who were long time residents in orthopedic department in the hospital, weren't enough. There was a deeper calling within me that would not be satisfied. I didn't quite know what it was and where it was going to take me. It was a calling I heard more clearly as years passed by. I left my job when I was expecting my first baby, knowing from the years I worked with patients, that their pain or *disabilities* were more complex than just physical, and I needed a new approach (to their *developing-abilities*) if I come back. I headed for my dream with more time on my hands.

I was born an artist like every other child born into this world.

Perhaps a life changing moment, which I had forgotten for many years, made me not give up on art like most kids did after some time.

After that moment, my self image was twisted against myself and my self-esteem was weakened. I became an introverted child. In my time alone, I loved to draw imaginary girls and women more and more. Who were they? An impression of myself, my mother, or any other woman? I didn't know. These portraits from my imagination, and then live portraits, won attention and later awards, but most importantly they brought me in close contact with human psyche at a very young age. Somehow they helped me see the beauty of the soul in everyone I drew.

In my early thirties, a few years after I quit my job, I started doing larger paintings and experimenting with compositions regardless of their subject. I attempted to let my subconscious mind lead as I put my attention only on unity and balance of the work. The paintings turned out to be imaginary still life and portraits. Portraits seemed to be pondering, with no lips, and gradually the top part of their head tended to drift out of the frame. I didn't quite get the message but my solo show raised a lot of questions for some visitors on why the portraits looked the way they did. I had no intention to tell any stories. I did not know until later that there was a story. It was my story, the one I did not know at the time.

After I had practiced and learned from a great *yoga* master who initiated my conscious life journey, I developed a view on the greater picture of life. I questioned myself as an artist; how could I value courage in my paintings by challenging a design for what my heart tells me, and not do so in my life. This felt like being dishonest to myself. I had to act the same in my life as I did in my paintings. I was deeply troubled at that time by a condition in my family life where I avoided conflicts as my only way to create peace. I gradually changed my response as I kept in mind what I learned in *ahimsa yoga*, and started redoing the composition of my life the way I did in my paintings. Here on the platform of life too, unity was the driving force and the elements of design were free to land anywhere as long as they had integrity and a meaningful relation to the whole picture. There was a strong resemblance of the actions and process, in both Life and in Art, and the pillars and guidelines of yoga were marvelously applicable and effective in both. There were deep links between *yoga* and *art*. After the first few years of change in my life setting, many facts started to reveal to me and there I noticed how my old paintings were pointing at these facts since long before. As I continued searching for the links, forty years were gone and the jubilee year came. I was released from the prison of the old misconception by remembering the childhood memory which was obscured all these years. I choose not to share the story because it involves other people. But I am grateful, regardless of the unnecessary pain I experienced throughout my life, for the opportunity it gave me to analyze and see in details something I truly loved. Meanwhile, art showed me how to see beauty where it was hard to foresee anything good.

This book is a prelude to a bigger art world within.

If you are an established artist you may find this book as an intellectual troubleshooting resource, finding out about what may hinder you from taking deeper joy in your work. And if you are a student it may direct you to your personal way from the very beginning of your experience in art. I intend not to offer a style, or even instructions for you to *invent* a style, (as all of this is possible) but a way to *find* your style in art, which reveals itself on the path to self-discovery. To the best of my ability, I have shared the main principles on how to center yourself on this journey, what you may face on the way, and how to handle it. I hope that as you read, you would see and feel more beauty around you and you would hear your heart more clearly than before. If you work with children, I hope after reading this book you would have more trust in their abilities in art and know the best way to guide them as they make their art.

As you read, you'll know why it matters a lot to take care of your body and your posture while doing art. Because body posture and mind gesture are parallel processes! As mind can reflect on body posture, the body posture can reflect back on the mind, therefore on your art.

You will know why it matters to identify your deepest intentions and to align them with a sense of love.

I avoided numbering and classifying when possible, so you instinctively use the talents of the right brain to grasp the concepts at your own pace. This will be helpful to develop artistic creativity.

Art exists beyond frames. It is not limited to talent or to skills and techniques. Its guidelines are in the heart. The ability to connect to a higher self, and to transform into one's best version, one's own truth, is inherited by every single being. Art has a shared ground for everyone, in all ages and positions in life, whether or not they believe they are an artist.

I hope you allow yourself to try it this way.

Chapter I

Beauty

Beauty

One of the great teachings that I learned as a young man was that looking at beauty in the world is the very first step in purifying the mind.

—Dr. Wayne Dyer
Podcast on Aug. 27, 2015

Being open to seeing beauty and comprehending it, is by itself a work of art. We're all lovers of the truth by our nature in however way we perceive the truth. This common love between all of us is the most beautiful connection that bonds us regardless of age, from east to west and north to south, and through millennia.

Truth has in it a character of beauty, whether completely hidden or slightly uncovered. As lovers of truth, each one of us searches for beauty in our own way. Glimpses of beauty that manifest here and there at times will give us a heart-warming message; the hope that we're not far from the truth. The fact is, our beloved is always by our side, only we leave it to search for it in other places.

The word beauty reminds each one of us of different images. Beauty can be identified in a variety of forms and realms, as everyone has different impressions about and experiences with it. What does the word beauty remind you of? Does it remind you of the blue sky? Or does it remind you of a flower, a landscape, or the ocean? Does it remind you of jewels found in the ocean made by the seashells? Or does it remind you of the jewels on the land shined and formed by hand? Do you find beauty in a sigh of relief that turns into a smile? Beauty appears in different depths, layers, and realms.

The best way to cultivate our sensibility to beauty is to start simply. Our senses should first familiarize themselves with how beauty feels. Paying attention to the most immediate visual or sound of beauty is a great way to start. Looking at or listening to the beauty in nature is easiest because our inner senses don't have to find out if they could trust its appearance. It's a transparent deal. Nature is already proven to be true and honest.

It is hard to wait for the perfect time or travel to the perfect place to see beauty in nature. It needs to be seen now and where you are. Paying attention, letting your feelings rise to admiration as you see the beautiful sky, the greens by the roads, the flowers, or the people you see every day is the way. This place of admiration is important because it guides you to gratitude even before you notice your blessings.

The atmosphere has oxygen that happens to reflect blue rays from sunshine. The trees recycle the oxygen back into the atmosphere, and they bring shade to their environment and house birds. How do they compose such beautiful, dynamic scenery every day, every hour, as they work hand in hand? I wonder.

The sky stands up so high for you to be in touch with it wherever you are. So stay in touch. Nurture your mind and soul through seeing the beauty of the world till you see the beauty that resides in you. It is the beloved that awaits your love.

Qualities of Beauty

Beauty manifests in all dimensions and many layers, not only one. When only one part looks beautiful, it overshadows the presence of other counterparts, and it's just a beautiful component. It's not integrated with the other components. True beauty has a deeper presence. True beauty is multidimensional and holistic. It forms as balance and charisma integrated in every layer, every dimension—one piece in relation to another, and both pieces in relation to the next, and all pieces in relation to the background. Once beauty manifests, it reveals yet another layer to harmonize with on a deeper level. And the story goes on.

Beauty, wisdom, love, courage, and stability are all different aspects of one concept even though we perceive them as different concepts or entities. We assign them to separate forms, like beauty in paintings, stability in architecture, and courage in a creative mind. But stability, wisdom, and courage are needed in a beautiful painting. Beauty in the physical world can't survive without strength and wisdom, and wisdom can't last long without bravery and beauty. Finally, none of them are born into the world of form and function in the absence of love, meaning compassion in a holistic manner.

True beauty comes with functionality, honesty, and innocence and has power, wisdom, and bravery in its core. *Beauty is holistic, dynamic, and integrated as a network woven with love, wisdom, innocence, and strength in all aspects of its presence.*

True beauty is meaningful. It relates to a greater structure of beauty and meaningful functions all throughout the surface, as well as in-depth layers. There is wisdom in beauty.

Beauty forms a network. The beauty is in the relationship of one to the other counterparts. If the beauty that shows up isn't connected to the network of the beauty, then it's a loosely floating concept that doesn't lead to any deeper truth. It's not connected to the whole. It's the meaning and the connection to the *network of beauty* that speaks the language of hearts. The meaning in beauty is neither in its subject nor in its theme. It lies in its kind presence.

This is true beauty. There are traces of true beauty everywhere, every day, and in every moment. We can develop our sensitivity to it and perceive more of it. We'll enjoy the outcome of sensing more beauty that leads to more inner peace and hope, even though our location and our time are still the same and nothing has changed in the world around us.

Look for beauty every day; practice actively probing for beauty. It's there, hidden but slightly revealed, waiting for you to find it. As you master the skill, you'll be able to see much more beauty in depth. But as a start, probe for nature's wonders every night and day. Seeing and paying attention to even a corner of the sky from a corner of a little window could open your heart. As beauty is multidimensional, it can be seen, heard, or just be deeply sensed by the heart.

As you practice noticing the beauty of the sky surrounding you, you'll see that beauty isn't only in the blue sky of the morning, but also in the red of the sunset. It's not only in the colorfulness of the sky but also in the gray sky that pulls itself back gently from the eyes, giving rise to other counter players to show you another form of beauty. *Beauty is dynamic.*

The tree has a different green today at 9:30 from yesterday at 9:30 when it was quite sunny. Everything else also looks different. It's a whole new composition even though everything is in the same place as yesterday. There's nothing new but a new beauty. *Beauty renews itself* or it's not beauty.

At night, though, when all colors subside into the dark, the absence of light opens the way for those who have always shone on but were hardly seen in the beam of sunlight or maybe behind the curtain of the clouds during the day. What a wonder every moment! As the days come by, for no reason of the season, they change. They play a new song. They play a new day in a new way, yet they keep the core rhythms unchanged. Silence and awe are what they summon.

All these rhythms of change also manifest in sound or touch. If you close your eyes, you'll hear the rhythms, feel the dynamism through the sounds of nature as the beauty manifests in every dimension. You can sense the breeze, the change of temperature, and the pressure of the wind on your face if your eyes are closed. You feel the air as it flows through your nostrils to your lungs.

To our subconscious mind, beauty is a translation for truth, and truth is a translation for love. Beauty isn't bound to a subject, nor to an object. *Beauty is boundless.* It lies everywhere in the hidden geometry, the relationships between the counterparts, and of the parts to the whole, and the whole to the truth to love. *Beauty isn*'t *about symmetry.*

In humans, beauty emanates from the source that lies in deep levels of existence. And any shells are around it. When they resonate with their inner truth, there will be no barrier for this beauty to become visible, or better said, sensible. And the beauty manifests. *Beauty isn*'t *bound to time and age.*

Have you seen the glow of this beauty on the faces of some people, regardless of how they look from the outside? They may have done something compassionate without even mentioning it to themselves or to others. Instead of remaining on the surface, the joy of the beautiful action was absorbed deeply and filled the heart. The beauty emanates from there. *Beauty isn't bound to forms, features, and numbers.* Beauty is boundless.

Beauty Must First Be Perceived to Become Alive

Beauty is born in the eyes of the lover when the lover meets with the beloved. Then the heart will gallop to reach the beloved, and the breath of joy follows and a journey to discovery begins. Masterpieces in museums can only give birth to their beauty when the eyes of their admirers see them.

The world of existence has always been harmonic, powerful, and balanced, but its beauty was never awed before the existence of humankind.

The eyes of a viewer with the presence of mind have an important role not only for nurturing the perceiver with beauty but also for the beauty itself to become alive. The elements of beauty exist everywhere in the world, but beauty doesn't become alive on its own. It must be seen, perceived, understood, and absorbed by the heart. Your heart is the place where beauty can become alive.

And the beauty will revive in perception.

Finding Beauty

But to look for the miraculous beauty of a rainbow, or the purple flowers covering a ranch, means you have to wait for the rain and sunshine to coincide, you have to wait for the springtime to travel to the perfect place to see the wonders of nature and get filled with joy and gratitude. On the other hand it means you hardly have a chance of seeing beauty at other times and around you, to feel the joy.

Of course, it's hard to find the extraordinary beauty of rainbows everyday because it isn't always available. But if it's not always there, instead there is miraculous beauty that is always around but is missed. It is the beauty that's always present but is left unnoticed on our everyday trip to work, to school, to shop or on our way back to where we rest. It is the beauty that appears every day from our window which we must see until we are ready to see the beauty inside.

Finding beauty around you will generate an intrinsic form of love that doesn't depend on any conditions, but one; your *readiness to sense beauty once you see it!*

When we are depressed, when disharmonies have frustrated us at a deep level, we disengage from what's around us as much as possible so as to not be affected again. (I hope you never disengage with yourself and never have to leave your own company.)

Often our other senses, receiving too many stimulants, can become insensitive, reduce engagements and become numb. This is also a natural physiologic reaction of nerve cells to pressure and prolonged stimulus. They accommodate. This is a way for our nervous system not to get shocked every time a traumatic event happens.

As our taste buds won't taste much flavor if they are given too much sugar, and as our ears would shut out sounds for a while after long exposure to high volumes, our emotions will also not be responsive after continuous exposure to harshness or unhappy situations, and we become depressed.

Our Senses Can Become Numb To Beauty

When senses partially quit engaging with the environment, it also impairs sensing the beauty and the natural intrinsic gratitude. Feeling that nothing is beautiful and worthy of praise is at first only a temporary and protective status of mind and emotions, but it may become a habit, a strict personal vision. It can become a door to depression if we believe that it has always been this way and it will always be.

Even if it had always been this way, it doesn't have to be so in the future. Life is like Beauty; it is dynamic and always ready to refresh and change, as beauty always renews itself.

The door to depression is the same door out of depression.

In this natural and common situation, a change of perspective can be the key to free yourself from chances of falling deeper into depression. When there are any disharmonies at your home, whether it's your physical home or the inner home that is the mind, acknowledge them but exclude them from your engagement with beauty. Don't let them in your mind at least for as long as you are practicing your sensibility for beauty. The disharmonies interfere and obstruct your senses to feel beauty.

Changing the spot where you eat, where you sleep every day, changing the sidewalk where you usually walk, sitting on the floor versus sitting at the table, can physically change your perspective to see from a different physical angle, so you can gain back your sensibility to beauty. Now you can see the physical world from a different angle and that's all you need for now. You are free. The beauty of the world is still pulsing. And everything is fine.

Start to probe for beauty, no matter how small or unimportant. You will gradually own back your sensitivity to the beauty around you, even though small but always precious. You will find your way through following this thread of beauty, to build a beautiful sacred place in your mind despite any disharmonies. Then as you move on noticing more beauty, you can survive the conditions, you can manage life better, and a wonderful change happens in you and around you.

A Practice To See Beauty:

It may be complicated to perceive all the beauty of the world at once. Let's practice on a flower in a pot. You admire the flower; for each petal, as you always did. Then probe for more. Look at the stem, how it has grown to hold the flower and to nourish it. Feel the stem down to the roots and the soil around it that secures it in place and feeds it. Look at the pot that holds the all of them ... Tune with the soul that's sitting still in front of you in peace.

Draw what you saw from memory. This way you will practice expanding the capacity of your visual memory in absorbing and holding love and beauty, not only to reproduce an image.

So ... do not count the petals, neither the leaves. Tune with them ... Let your heartbeat count them for you.

Change Your Perspective To See More Beauty

If you were to enter earth today and engage with the air and the earth, you wouldn't know the trees and the sky and the clouds. You would just see them, wondering why does life has to be so beautiful here? That's how you feel when you change your perspective! It's like the delight you feel when you free yourself from a nightmare by simply waking up.

You can do it by looking at the sky, the clouds, the birds, the sea and the earth with all the trees as if you've seen them for the first time. You can save yourself from sadness by opening your eyes to the available beauty by your side.

Perspective in visual arts is seeing things from the point in space where your eyes are. This point can change as you move through space. In the inner world perspective is seeing a subject from your place in the realm of thoughts.

When you practice visual art, like drawing or photography, what you see looks different as you change your location. Look at a refrigerator, a big box, or a street from one point of view. Then change your point of view by changing where you stand. Go to the other corner and see it, sit on the ground and look from a lower level, go higher on the steps, or further from your subject: you will see it differently each time. This is usually taught by some line formulas in visual arts that are often learned as templates. But this fact cannot be absorbed by the heart if you don't discover it yourself. This is a life-enhancing lesson that the discovery brings you. It practically shows you that things seem different when we change our viewpoints in life.

There is a Zen quote that Dr. Wayne Dyer often mentioned: *when you change the way you see the world, the things you see will change.*

But real proof for this change comes only after you try it and see it for yourself.

You will find yourself in the peacefulness that you have created by simply seeing the slightest beauty. You will actually emanate and create impressions of peacefulness on the world around you, which would reflect back on you like a mirror.

TO SEE

Seeing beauty happens inside you, not just in your physical eyes, but also in your inner eyes, and in the background of your mind. Seeing beauty brings you to a state of gratitude for what is, and can soothe your heart.

Seeing is also the key to making a perfect work of art.

The word *seeing* points at a deep and precise view of the realities in the inner or the outer world. But where does it happen? Does it need physically open eyes?

Open eyes are only one of the gates. Seeing an image does not happen in the eyes, and neither on the retina; the screen in the depth of the eyeball where the image is projected. But the light of the image travels to the visual area of the brain in the occipital lobe in the rear part of the brain. There will still be two slightly different upside down images, each one from a slightly different angle! The rest of the process of perception seems like mystery.

How we see an upright image, from the inverted image, is what happens only in the beginning of the mysterious path of seeing. In fact physical seeing happens with integration of a lot of other senses. True *seeing* is seeing through the wisdom that interprets all of the integrated sensory data. It is the gate to an *inner eye.* No matter where or which direction you look, outward to the world, or inward to your inner realm, you can have a sense of beauty, a vision, an image that may be interconnected by a sense of a taste, a smell, a sense of motion, or a sound. You may as well hear a melody that forms an image and a vision in your mind.

You can see beauty as you listen to it and you can listen to beauty as you see it.

Seeking Beauty

Seeking the most beautiful of all is not through comparison of flowers to each other. It is not even in comparison of flowers to beautiful trees, that the most beautiful of all can be discovered in nature! The *most beautiful* resides in the wavering forms of the flowers and the trees as they still hold unity in the core of their being, in the way they live. They all breath, nourish, and flourish by air, water and light through their vessels. The march of the plants towards sunlight, anywhere in the world, is the unity among their diverse shapes and kinds.

Beauty resides in the infinite ways that sameness can show up in variable forms!

Beauty is the invisible harmony and oneness found in the core of variety.

It is what co-ordinates everything, which is always present and felt by hearts. Sometimes it manifests through visible forms and sounds. Sometimes it remains dormant, quietly hidden. The search for beauty is a story of hide and seek that you play. It is the joyful game of life. (The game is sometimes taken more seriously than seeing the beauty of the life itself.)

Beauty Resides Within Relationships

It is not found by the comparison of a part to its counterparts. It is found by looking at its *harmonious placement* among the other parts.

Now consider the relation of the visible beauty and its beautiful presence, to the state of its non-existence in the past. Here is born another form of deeper beauty.

Beauty is found through comparison of the flower to its

absence in the past or future. It is in the wonder of how the chances came together to make it happen for the flower to be here!

Beauty resides in the relation of existence to non-existence. What brings meaning to the non-existence, and defines the existence is beautiful.

Beauty is in the Wisdom Hidden in Nothingness That Shifts the Non-Being to the State of Being

Beauty is in the rhythms of your pulse, between every breath you take. It is in the existence of the flower in each moment after another, as it changes moment to moment.

Beauty exists in the relationships of the bits that conform to make something, and their manifestation and remission, in the world.

The beauty of a flower is not only in its colors and shapes but also in its bloom and fall, and its rise to bloom, and the silence in between.

On the path to cultivate our senses to recognize beauty, we might notice *pseudo beauty*. There are things that seem harmonic in the surface level, but don't have a link to the deepest levels. Pseudo beauty usually points in one direction and distracts from other dimensions of beauty, like wisdom and functionality. If you look at pseudo beauty from those other aspects of beauty, no beauty is sensed. Pseudo beauty will not eventually satisfy the deep burning love for the truth. (An example will be in the next paragraph).

Still, falling in disappointing love with pseudo beauty can introduce you to *your own loving nature* and yearning for beauty and truth, and the beautiful fact that you are already *in love.*

Semi beauty on the other hand, is the beauty that starts to appear in one dimension and can evolve to other dimensions and become holistic, but it has not conformed to its own truth yet. It is on its way to completion.

Imagine a home you want to buy, that is in process of remodeling. When you see it, it has the front door finished, the entrance looks great, there are some new tiles, and a new sink inside, but the paint and the cabinets are not done yet. The location is great and the foundation of the home, too. It is on its way to become completely favorable both in function and appearance. This portrays a bit of semi beauty, which is on its way to become beauty.

If the home looks wonderful and completely finished from a distance, but in a closer look, and by touching the walls, it becomes clear that the whole home is made of cardboard, then it is not a real home to live and shelter in, even though it is beautiful and spacious! That is like pseudo beauty, which only creates an illusion of beauty while it is far from it.

Your senses may have also looked into a disharmony in disguise; a beautiful appearance that sparkled on behalf of the ultimate beauty of the truth inside, but later there was no connection to support the relation of the inner and outer beauty. You may have experienced it in intimate relationships, or in a big decision in your life. It can be frustrating.

There is a choice; to train the senses, percept a deeper kind of beauty, the one that exists in the relationships between the *beauty of existence*, and the *beauty of performance*.

Beauty of performance or of kind actions is the connection between the apparent beauty and the beauty of the truth inside.

Search wisely. Outer level beauty is not always a manifestation of the inner beauty and truth, it may only be the reflection of the standards of beauty by trends of the day, which changes from time to time. Beauty is neither bound to subjects and objects, nor bound to time.

What Beauty is, is always beautiful. Beauty is not a temporary value.

When searching for beauty, see if the outer beauty resonates with the inner true beauty. This resonance must be made before inner true beauty could be seen from outside.

Praise the beauty in the core being of individuals and the efforts they make to manifest it. Ponder the manifested: whether it is a reflection of the mind or it emanates from the core.

True beauty is generated in actions and in thoughts. Seeking beauty has adventures and challenges until you find the beauty that is the truth. It is the beauty that is beyond the reach of the five senses. But the heart *can* detect it. Hearts hold the essence of true beauty in them, a reference point that is Love. This is why disharmony hurts the heart, and the beauty heals it.

This form of beauty can be constantly generated virtually between you and your environment. This is the one that you create like a painting, based on principles of design. You can create a fine connection between your outer and your inner beauty through what you do, how you think and how you interact with the world around you. This is the greatest art you could create on the planet.

The beauty you find in the sky, in the rivers and the mountains, in the trees and in all nature, is yours. It is a reflection of the deep beauty in you, so enjoy it, admire it and treasure it. Seek the beauty outside of you till you see the beauty, the seat of love, in you.

Beauty in Motion (Human Gait)

Just like the visual beauty we sense from the outside world, our inner senses can perceive beauty inside. As they perceive, more beauty is born.

The tree leaves move by the winds, but many kinds of living things in the world move actively. Some fly, some crawl, some walk. Active movements are possible on a base of support where gravity works to the benefit of balance and forward thrust during the movement. The balance is naturally more secure on a wider base of support with the weight closer to the ground, like that of a crocodile, or a tiger. Ants with their light body need less energy to move than the alligators!

The lesser the base of support and the higher the center of gravity, the more balancing work falls within the responsibility of the one who moves. The further from the ground, the harder it is to keep the line of gravity of the body securely in the base of support on the ground. Having four feet on the ground makes it possible for the very tall giraffes to keep balance in movements.

How can humans walk so gracefully only on two feet with a small base of support relative to the height?

How integrated must the human neuromuscular system be to talk while walking with other tasks on hand, and still keep the body from falling, as the weight shifts from one leg to another in every step?

Human gait, the simple act of walking, is one of the wonders of the world. We walk, run, and work on the least base of support that is as wide as our feet and the distance between them on the ground.

In every step we are about to fall but an involuntary and highly equipped system puts us back up right without grabbing our attention!

You can have an idea of your position and your location in mind, even when your eyes are closed. Now if your position changes as the eyes are still closed, you can still keep track of the changes through a deep sensory system that will let you know of your new condition in space. This deep perception notifies the brain about the position of the body in the air at each moment, according to gravity.

While walking with open eyes, through both types of external five senses and deep internal sensory system, the brain is notified of the position and location of every limb, comparable to the patterns of motion that are intended. It sends the command as an impulse to the muscles that must take action. Thus, you move, you walk to the table perhaps to grab a glass of water, and as you think of the water, all other neuromuscular pathways are in favor of getting you there without falling.

In every shift of weight from one leg to the other, movements of the trunk and the hips take place in ways that balance the weight on the legs, which are changing position rhythmically as they swing and land on the foot. And in the middle of this rhythm, your knee is the beautiful shock absorber. It locks and embraces the load of the body when the heel touches the ground, and it unlocks after the shift of weight is complete.

As one group of muscles gradually releases the foot to the ground, the counter group gradually picks up the heel and pushes for the next step. The arms swing as well to help with the balance of the body but they are also on call, so when you reach the table you can have your water.

As you walk, the muscle contractions follow patterns of impulses from the brain and it's the *sequence* of the contractions that matters. This sequence, that resembles an orchestra, keeps you upright and tuned like a symphony as you walk. It makes the best choices in every shift of weight to promote your body in a direction. It prevents a fall as gravity is always at work to pull the body down. It aligns your body in a way that instead of falling prey to gravity, gravity becomes a supporter that will secure the skeletal structures on top of each other.

Like a majestic tower in motion, in wondrous balance, floating in air in each step taken forward, and landing on the ground safe, and safe again on the least base of support, human walks high against all the odds of gravity.

Isn't such harmony so beautiful?

Who taught you to walk so gracefully?

What a harmony and timing should be at work between the impulses from the nervous system and the exact group of muscles that are in action at one moment but not the next!

The next moment, they must *let go* of a contraction and gently come to relax in order to let another group of muscles to come into play, and if they don't let go, there will be a rigid stillness instead of movement.

No movement will take place despite all the efforts in muscles, if they all insist on continuing to act after their part is done.

At times when the body needs to adopt a crutch or prosthesis as a new support to create balance again, the harmony between the brain and musculoskeletal system enters a new level. It changes a default pattern of gait that has been inherited and developed through many years, and turns it into a custom made pattern to meet the new necessities of gait.

Through hard work, it creates new sequences, new rhythms of motion that build integrity and harmony between all parts of the body again, so the body can still have stability and mobility!

The nervous system changes its pathways to do the best possible job in keeping daily activities on track.

The nervous system is a highly creative gift. If we choose to delegate the tasks of this creative system to our logical mind, which may be filled with knowledge of anatomy, physics, chemistry, biomechanics and neurology, we may not walk in a minimal level of such harmony and such creativity. Because thinking of *how*, *when* and *which* will block the natural pathways of the highly creative system. This system communicates in the form of a web between the cerebellum, the brain and the body and naturally comes up with a lot of solutions in times of need. *We all have it. Our job is to keep the desire to walk and not lose hope on the way.*

This seems like the same system that with practice, helps you play the violin, draw lines, paint, as well as re-balance yourself when you navigate through life.

Isn't this beautiful?

The Bond

Muscles contract after the sequence of impulses from the brain but still, they cannot move a finger alone. A muscle cannot do without the bone! And the two can't do it without a tendon to bond them together!

Our muscles, bones, and nerves have an amazing potential to be functional. But if they are not connected, they cannot make the slightest movement, let alone walk and run.

The connective tissue that bonds them, is like a matrix that changes form to become a tendon, or loosens to pass nutrients to the cells. It is a loving ground of existence that feeds every cell of our physical body, and harmonizes them in every act to make our desires achievable.

Maybe this connective matrix, the common and loving ground, exists among humans too.

Beauty and Ego

If the world of being is created by divine love, it is hard to believe that ego in its original form is rooted in anything other than love.

Ego is the love for the *self.* It supports the minimal *self* on its path of growth to a *vast understanding of self.*

The love for *self* is an early stage of love which protects individuals from danger and secures survival and growth by recognizing the boundaries at every physical, emotional and spiritual level.

Perhaps, at first ego loved only the *self.* Then as the *self* recognized the love for another, the ego became the love for *two.* As the two formed a family, the self expanded and so ego was to support the survival boundaries of *the family,* and as the understanding of *self* expanded, the individual's ego adopted its *community* and *beyond,* in its *self love.*

Ego at the healthy functional level holds the mechanism that motivates you to have a good diet and good sleep habits, to treat yourself fairly, to give up work when you are too tired, and to flee when you feel danger.

This simple self-care system is a built in system similar to the pattern of protective reflexes in the nervous system which keep you from falling, protecting the head from any trauma, and so on.

It is only when the ego as a function is assumed as an identity, and when it is mistaken with the true self, that problems arise.

I truly know how precious it is to have a healthy ego developed naturally in childhood because I had a weak and unsupportive ego for many years of my life.

If I were verbally attacked, I would doubt myself instead of defending myself.

And the blame and the shame would be mine.

There is nothing wrong with the healthy functions of ego.

All suggestions and advice you hear of taming the ego (as if it's wild), overriding and letting go of it (as if it is not needed at all), are because ego is mindless.

Yes, ego is mindless, but not heartless. It is born of love, but a shortsighted one.

Because ego is mindless, it needs to be guided as its natural life goes on. *Ego's natural life is to thin out and expand further, to extend its love, as awareness grows.*

As ego stretches further along with awareness, it seems as if its shells become less dense, and more translucent, and finally transparent enough to allow a far-sighted view! That's how you develop empathy and feeling for others, and love for the entire life on earth.

Until reaching that perfect view, there are great teachings and good advice available that can help one avoid the harmful mistakes of running on a short-sighted device.

The disabling emotions that may paralyze the ego or stop it from expansion are fear, greed, and hatred. They do not originate from love. How can they ever feed the ego and expand it? The ego remains immature under the influence of fear, greed and hatred.

When negativity is allowed to grow on the ego and take over its space and natural function, it becomes harmful to others and that's when the taming and letting go is suggested. But living with less than a healthy ego harms you by malnutrition, chronic fatigue or a broken heart.

Like the blue atmosphere around the earth that supports life on earth, so is a healthy ego surrounding and supporting you. The atmosphere filters the sunlight and lets the right amount of light in. Any shooting star coming from space to the boundaries of the atmosphere will naturally burn off before it hits the ground, yet the atmosphere does not do the same to space.

There is such beauty in ego.

Still, there is a deeper kind of beauty in you which is like a compass in your life journey. It is worth exploring the beauty in you.

Chapter II

Art

ART

Art is the state of being. Being here ... where you are.

Your being here is the outcome of many forces and factors that happened to align, and led to your presence here, against all odds of random forces that could do otherwise!

This is Art of the Divine. It is gifted to living things.

If you fully attend to your presence here at this moment, you will see the state of art in your presence.

But often our bodies are here and our minds, somewhere in the past or future. And the beauty of the simply being here is missed.

The art of humans as conscious beings is to choose a way back to this blissful moment and place of presence that was gifted.

This way passes through the contrasts and opposites.

Entering the bliss of this moment is not always through meditative stillness. It often requires a dynamic state of mind, requires actions and thoughts to undo the unnecessary, within the moment. Entering the bliss of the moment is simply doing what's best and kindest to do at this moment, even if it is only to keep breathing in silence, just because this is the best thing to do at the time.

There is an accomplishment in doing this best in each moment. And the best is not often what we expect it to be.

Only the art of humans as conscious beings is what we refer to as *Art* in this book.

Art is Born of Passion for Beauty

Art is born of the passion and love for beauty, and it reflects the same qualities it has longed for once it is matured.

Art manifests in tangible and non-tangible forms, through creativity. Art can dance like beauty, can sing like beauty, art imitates beauty in the physical world through creative work. The two pillars for the bridge the creative process needs are the *mind* and the *body.*

Paintings, symphonies, sculptures and all what we call art are just manifestations of art. Art itself is not visible to the eyes. It's not hearable by the ears. It is only felt by inner senses in the heart, and in every cell. Art is the one that gives you chills. Wherever art happens, the inner senses become united, and healing begins.

Art resides independently within but beyond the art piece. The piece can contain the art like a vessel that holds the content. Art could fill in a painting, a piece of music, the story of a play, the shapes and structures, or a life story, like water filling a vessel, if it will. *Art will not remain in cracked vessels, which are made with motives that are bonded and formed by less than love.*

Art in any form is a natural consequence of *passionate* and *compassionate* thoughts and acts of *wisdom* and *honesty.*

Thus true art is born of true intentions of kindness, fairness within the dynamics of different rhythms, be it the notes and silences, spaces and objects, colors and lines, or a simple and honest word in the midst of confusion.

The Realm of the Arts

Art can manifest in two ways: the way that our five sensory organs can detect, and a way beyond the five sensory perceptions.

If it is going to be perceived by the five sensory organs, it needs a vessel, a vehicle to hold it and carry it to the physical world of sounds, tastes and shapes or colors. This vessel is the *art form.* Every art form has some *art techniques, tools* and a quality called *craftsmanship* to perform it. In every painting, every piece of music, every sculpture, there are some techniques, tools and craftsmanship used.

But not anywhere that art techniques, tools and craftsmanship are applied will art exist. It exists only where love, wisdom, and unity are in the nature of the work.

We have deeper senses to detect beauty and we have more ways to create art accordingly. *Art has a larger kingdom to show up in.*

What you do when you live a life, when you intend to find your way through both realms of inner and outer world and still keep your integrity, you are invisibly creating art. Once you do it passionately with love, in a way that is balanced, fair and kind to yourself and others, it is then a masterpiece.

Passion

The passion for art comes from the spiritual aspect of passion before it manifests at a physical level.

The passion for life adventures comes also from the same spiritual aspect of this source of energy.

Passion at a physical level is the sexual energy provided for the survival of all species. This sacred energy sustains the *survival* of all species as wide as the planet, and as long as eternal time through the offspring. It also *revives* the inner life force by reviving memories of eternal time within the boundaries of this moment.

This energy fuels the journey to birth in a vast area, birth of new people, birth of new ideas, new view points and the birth of all solutions that have the content of life and love in them.

If you recall a creative moment in your life and you have a deeper look at this memory, you may remember how you happened to create. There must have been something that put you in awe for a moment, you felt deeply astonished, and your heart started pounding as if you had just heard of your beloved. You got inspired; you felt you are in love with something you can hardly put a name on. You carried the promise then with you, fully committed wherever you went, until it was matured enough to appear outward and to be delivered to the world.

When our senses encounter true beauty, they perceive it. They fall in love within a spark of time. The passion ignited with this love is the fire that fuels the journey of life. The life of a new vista, the life of a new piece. The newly born vista appears through various sensory or deep sensory venues. The result is music, architecture, visual arts, theatrical arts, culinary arts, fashion design, or the great art of navigating tirelessly through life mazes without hurting anyone or anything including yourself.

The realm of true love and passion is holistic so it has a sphere of implications.

-In one way it is love for all *living things.*

-In another way love is projected on *life* itself.

The love for all *living things* is compassion for all including yourself. The mind interprets this love as two different components: compassion for self versus compassion for others. The presence of the ego as a self-protective mechanism causes this duality at some levels of awareness.

The love for *life* gives birth to a sense of deep gratitude for the chance of being alive.

It gives birth to a sense of admiration, the awe and wonder for life.

It also gives birth to a deep burning passion for seeking and knowing. Science and art are born from this love.

The love and passion to seek and to know brings the *courage* to step on the path that the beloved shows you, regardless of the fear inside.

Have you ever thought you have lost your passion or wondered if you ever had any?

You do have a passion in life.

At any place in the sphere of love you find yourself, from there you can emanate your love in all directions.

And from whichever corner you enter the sphere, you are *in.*

In fact, you are *in love.*

The point is we all vibrate in and out of the sphere of love from time to time, until we locate our unique place in it.

Creativity

We can't *create* anything from scratch. We can't do such magic of bringing anything new to this world all by ourselves. Even the most innovative ideas have potentially been here already, but invisibly.

The things we can bring to the world are wishes that we make, inspired by love. We can only long for something, keep a deep desire and tune ourselves with it, get inspired by it again and again, and intend to find a perspective closer to the beloved. It is that desire, and the courage to make the shift to a new perspective, that actualizes the potential new idea through a creative process.

We can only fall in love, make a wish and keep the wish alive, all by ourselves, a complete wish made from scratch.

We can keep the flame of our desire burning without help from anyone or anything. We are the only one who can set light to this desire and let it burn for years in the darkness of confusion.

This is the true flame of passion that glows in all kinds of love you have experienced from childhood to parenthood, from a career passion, to a passion for exploring life at the cost of letting go of a career. You can create a new vision, which gives birth to new ways and new ideas of how to walk along the stormy paths of life without losing the flame inside.

Creativity is often mistaken for art or an artistic product. Artistic product is the sensory form of art, like a painting, a sculpture, or music ... that is made through a creative process.

But the zest to carry the impression of beauty to the physical world is creativity.

Creativity is the energy that brings the innovation from a virtual state of mind to reality.

Nothing can really be created except new wishes, new visions, thus new responses and actions. Everything else has been and will be. Creativity is also in keeping your new vision, in balance between your system and the world around you. Creativity is like making new mind gestures, like a surfer's posture that changes and renews according to the waves. And creativity seems like an ongoing mode of life that exists beyond surfing.

The world inside and the world outside both change constantly. In each moment, either the mind and emotional status change, or the conditions of the outside world change. Creativity acts in every move you make in shifting to the new condition!

A surfer tunes with the creativity that exists in the spirit of waves. The creative spirit of waves lives in each and every drop of water, and the surfer's movements symbolize it.

Creativity moves every drop of water, along roads of the river or heights of the waves, making nothing out of nothing but balance out of initial *balance.*

The water on a river may slow down but may not stop. There's always a new path for the drop of water to go; down in the ground, up in the sky, back to the ground and moving forward, whichever makes best sense for the moment. That's creative. And that's what the surfer practices, being one with the spirit of creativity in every drop of water, the drop that yields into an inner change in respect to the outer change, to come to *balance.*

When the passionate surfer stands still on the land, watching the heightened waves in the storm without joining them, it is greatly creative as well. For the surfer knows that this is time for the waves to perform alone. So the surfer would let water be the only dancer on the stage.

The way to keep your balance in the midst of these changes is creativity.

Your status, as a result of your efforts, is the artistic product where beauty manifests.

And you are the artist.

There are times when you have the skills of doing art, you have love for what you do but there is no zest to do it. Do not worry that you may have lost your wings.

At those times some *potentiality* is increasing. Creativity is working somewhere else in your life, finding another venue. Do you know why creativity looks for another venue?

Because circumstances change, times change, necessities change, and creativity can only work in the callings of the *now.*

Your life has a lot of aspects and venues for creativity. The more you cultivate your creativity through art, the more powerful creativity works in other aspects of your life.

The art that is created may be within a format of music or visual arts or it may be formless. So creativity doesn't always lead to a tangible product. At times, it leads to a solution that solves many problems at once! Only remember not to bind your creativity to only one venue.

Creativity is construction of new paths of thinking. That path is paved in the mind of the thinker. It may not have a weight or a measurable mass but it is surely made. A highway between senses, between the logical and the inspirational areas of mind, to team up their activities in a way to reach a higher view, rather than challenge each other. Looking at the art that is made after the new path of thinking inspires the viewer or the perceiver to create a new way of thinking, to find solutions for the same old problems that seemed to be irresolvable.

Creativity is that zest to find the best way to do things in the moments given (as the present time).

If your focus is on love, beauty and kindness, what your creativity carries to life will be art.

If the focus on love is missed for the focus on fear, the solutions creativity brings will be based on fear, which is not a perfect solution in the long run, but just a temporary fix.

So creativity is the zest to take action, not the outcome of the action. Every art is the outcome of creativity but not every creative process leads to art. Art comes from the place of love and all kinds of passion: compassion for all, and self-compassion.

When attention is on a mirror image of love, which is exactly opposite of love, what creativity brings to life will resemble art but will not function like art, and will not feel like art. Let's call it **pseudo-art**.

There fall all the techniques that employ one's best energies, in service for something that is void of love and beauty, and has no joyful rewards.

In this way creativity still works in the *now*, but in absence of truth and love for true beauty, creativity reduces an artistic way of life to an opportunist way of living.

Dark Arts and Bright Arts

In fictional stories, what is known as the dark arts is the art which is done without the light of awareness. The awareness of love.

There is nothing scary or supernatural about it and you need not be afraid of any dark arts even in your imagination.

Our subconscious mind has a common code for perception of the physical world. It is not a man-made code or sign, and does not need to be learned or taught.

In its language, light is recognized or perceived as consciousness or awareness.

Absence of light is recognized as absence of awareness, as a definition of the unknown, the unfamiliar.

In reverse, when the subconscious mind does not know something or some realm, it perceives an absence of light, which is called darkness.

In reality when there is no light in a space, the objects that seem dark at the time, might be just as bright as light objects when the light is projected on them.

This is also true with awareness. The difference is not in the nature of the dark or light space. It is only about sensing the presence of our awareness as the light projected on and reflected back from them.

What this light has not projected on, does not reflect it back so it seems dark. Once it does receive light, it will be bright too.

Using knowledge of art principles and techniques as tactics in life is not a wise application of art. Since every art technique comes from the kingdom of love, they all work under the same rule as well. Without this awareness, art is done in absence of light.

An act based on absence is based on something that does not exist, which is called *nothing*. This action, even though skillfully done, is considered the *nothing* in the kingdom of love where we all rooted from. It will not pay off as much as it has been worked for. Therefore the dark art cannot promote anyone to anywhere unless the awareness projects light on it.

The awareness is not knowing more and more details of specifics techniques and tactics. It is the knowing about the whole and its matrix.

In this matrix, the knowledge and techniques are only tools, and art happens when a great *wisdom* balances the work that's done by the tools. The wisdom is the *wisdom of love.*

There is no secret to know but the *rule of love.*

The work pays off when in love, service and selflessness.

What dark arts truly are can simply turn into *bright arts* in the presence of this awareness.

You as the Viewer of Art

The Importance of You as the Perceiver of the Art

The beauty that manifests in an art product is not yet as vibrant as it was seen by the artist.

That beauty awaits the moment to be re-discovered by the eyes of the viewer to become alive again.

Know that you have an important role in bringing art to life not only when you practice art but also when you are looking at art. You allow the beauty to survive and thrive in the artwork you like.

When you are touched by an artwork, you have a special place in the life of that artwork. The place is for you because the art in that piece cannot live itself without making sense, without creating a deep feeling and a profound meaning. You are where those senses are made and those meanings are created. The artwork's life journey is never complete without you, the viewer. *You are part of the artwork you like.*

So many times you go to a museum to see art, while those pieces that you think are finished pieces are there to make a new art as you walk by them.

As you get inspired, and you decide to renew your points of view, this new art takes place in you.

Language of Visual Arts

Visual art is a delicate language. Maybe that is why it's called fine art! The language points out the existing inner or outer realities, gives you hints, but never points it out directly. Instead, the direct encounter with the realities happens internally in the viewer's mind.

When you see a painting, you get a feeling of balance or imbalance based on a sense of weight! The entrance door of visual art is through the eyes, but from the entrance it immediately connects to deep senses of balance, weight, density, sound, heat and so on. The connection is based on memory of physical experiences retained in the subconscious mind. Active colors in terms of chroma and darker tones of the colors feel heavier. Lines can also make you sense some instability if they are vertical or at a mild angle. In paintings or interior design, horizontal lines and forms feel more secure. Visual arts feel quite mechanical and the cerebellum is probably very much engaged in not only three dimensional (3D) visual arts, like sculpture, but also in two dimensional (2D) visual arts, like paintings.

The sensory data received by the subconscious mind from looking at a painting can also provoke a sense of taste or music.

The point is that artwork is a sensory stimulant that activates many integrated senses in the brain. This activation can lead to much deeper sensory and memory levels where there's a personal and unique symbolic language. In the mind of the viewer, it may convey an aspect of beauty beyond words; a meaning and sense that even the artist was not consciously aware of at the time of creating the piece.

Art Making

Art is the alignment of physics, biology, psychology, and math coming together to make a statement of love.

This statement is not in the subject, neither in the story, nor on the stage, but behind the scene. Behind the scene is where the elements of art bond together to form a multidimensional message of love and unity, not a message of fear and hopelessness.

Art making in nature is not making a line of production out of the similar findings that are already approved by the collective art culture. It is not something expected and predictable.

Art making doesn't aim for adding more bodies of artwork, more paper and more mass to the world, or astonishing people, breaking records and being exceptional.

Art making is a kind of scientific research and study in the art world. The outcome is not predictable. In art making, The *known* is utilized to search for the *unknown.*

Art making is to nurture the questions of each and every individual mind that eventually elevate the collective culture to another level far ahead. Art making is a matter of giving birth to ideas whose time to live has arrived. These ideas have a virtual body that every artist carries a bit of into the world.

Art symbolizes the life journey of the mind of humankind. This collective life journey creates the currents of cultures that start with a pure intention, and elevates the norms beyond the anticipated levels.

Practicing art is practicing a version of life's games in form of shapes and colors, sounds and silences that relate to each other, to create rhythms and harmonies, and to bond the particles to become one whole, a whole story to make sense...only to create a moment of reflection. The reflection that provides an outlook which makes a difference in choices we make in life.

Art and the Art Industry

Industries have predefined goals and protocols. Their market and values are within the physical realm and often ready and within reach.

Art as a creative and scientific quest has other qualities.

Its destination is in the non-physical world and cannot be pre-defined, even if its path is defined.

It may also have very little or no value in the market at the time of its birth into the physical world.

A while after the creative investigation brings some new idea worthy of attention to the world, even though the industry is doubtful of investing in it, commercial arts and craft masters may like the idea, adopt it, reproduce it, and promote the idea in different forms and varieties in the mass market.

The new artistic idea would be trending and the industries now pick it up (like poster or T-shirt companies) which is vital to the life of the new idea that the art has brought forth to the era.

The transmission of the new art ideas to the collective artistic mind of the society was made possible by commercial art industries!

Even though the art industry has not directly brought forth the new idea, it has had an impact on the life journey of this new idea in the world. The art industry has an important role of choosing what to reproduce. It transcends the new values and viewpoints to the vast mind of the society, the new vista that was found by artists and seekers of no industry!

This new idea, this change of the viewpoint, which was born after a creative and non-judgmental investigation, belongs to the people of its time and the times after. Its life journey and tests are possible only when it is among the people.

From the birth of the new art idea to its trending in the mass market, artists, craft masters, and the industry work together like a chain. If each work is done with pure intentions of love, the chain becomes a beautiful necklace on the cultural body of their time that stands out in art history.

Attachment and Release

Sometimes an artist quest leads to a new style that can have an immediate market in a community. The artist may decide to promote the newfound idea by reproducing it repeatedly in a variety of forms, but he or she can also become attached to this idea and eventually stop his or her own journey in art.

The reverse may happen for someone working in the art industry who may be inspired by a quest for an art journey where there will be no visible market or reward at the end. (It will be a brave act of *release* of a socially successful routine that is emotionally non-rewarding.)

Because of the dynamic nature of life, we need not be attached to any artistic idea that has become a successful trend now.

By the time the new artistic ideas start trending, their time too, *shall pass*! The necklace is already complete.

The arts that are trending now are attuned with the callings of a time in the past when they were born. We don't need to follow them for so long. We could move on and tune into the callings of the *now*, where creativity can perform again.

Art Spirit

Popular trends retain the shells of the new idea as it was first manifested in the public eye. The new idea itself, though, transforms and leaves the shells. It lends its pieces to creativity for another round.

Art in its true nature is like a kind and loving wisdom in

a system that is run by the minds and hearts in centuries. It carries various tasks in each era in history and in various parts of the globe; an era of change or renaissance, a time for narrative reflection of the events, a time to release of toxic residues of anger and violence and even a time for clarifying the doubts about art itself. All of the jobs lead to the healing of emotional wounds, and clarifying visions, so the minds and the culture of human can bloom again.

Art never clings to one job and one form. As times change, the needs and necessities of the societies' mind change, and so should the work of this intellectual service to humankind.

Through narrative art in paintings, poetry, music and theater, awareness of what's happening in the world was brought to people throughout centuries. Painting scenes that tell the story of an event, story of violence or stories of a life journey lead these stories to travel from culture to culture, from one point in time to another when visual documentation by photography was not available and there was no immediate connection throughout the world by travel and phone.

In today's world, news of events runs through a system that employs all art techniques; it is fast, worldwide and documental for future generations.

What was left from the legacy of telling the story of events has found its way into fiction and entertainment art. Violence has a special place in it. This style opens our eyes to the realities of the past, not the necessities of the now, so we miss out on the real times.

Is there any good in watching yesterday's sad realities while today we can initiate the better realties we want to happen tomorrow?

What the world needs is not the art that echoes the same narrative language of fear and alarming shocks to awaken us. It is to bring another form of awareness. The awareness of what lies behind all these dramas in life; knowing that still, there is a blue sky behind the clouds. Knowing that there is hope and everyone has power to heal at least one wounded heart on the planet, and that a better tomorrow can be as real as the sad yesterday.

In old times, care givers and educators used fear of future to motivate learning in young learners.

This technique of bringing awareness in art is as outdated as those old ways of teaching kids! Why learn by experiencing pain when we can learn through inspiration, wisdom and motivation by beauty?

You Don't Have to Always Learn the Hard Way

Sometimes tactics of targeting the emotions are used to make a point. Using sound and visual effects the viewer's emotions is compelled to arise.

But the viewer, the audience must have a choice, must be free to feel what they normally tend to feel.

Attracting the attention of the audience should not be forceful. Neither is bringing awareness possible by activating fear, hatred and anger in the audience, nor are fear, hatred, and anger good entertainers.

Once the violent scenes are used as amusements and the audience is drawn into this attraction, the nervous system has to adapt to it in order to handle the shocks. This is how the sense of a normal speed or the sense of danger gets numb; senses of compassion have to be suppressed for a while in order to let one watch an amusing horror movie with lots of violence and lost lives in the story.

Following the trend of violence in any form of art may become popular, but it impairs the sense of safety or danger for both the artist and the audience.

As a viewer, watching violence can also spread a misleading fear. The sense of empathy, if it has not been numbed yet, causes a feeling of danger while watching the horror movie. You may tune into the fictional story in a way that there is no barrier between you and the one who gets hurt. The mind retains the memory of what it has received through the eyes ears and all sensory receptors, and interprets the data in connection with what happened in that condition. In other words, the mind becomes conditioned according to what it is usually exposed to. Watching violent or horror fictions increases sensibility to danger and creates a form of fear and apprehension of situations that resemble what was seen in the movie, just as a protective mechanism. This happens unconsciously. This momentarily apprehension and fear can build a pattern of fear, while it is not at all realistic. You would be living in unnecessary fear.

Watching horror or violence as entertainment may also lead to loss of sensitivity to loud sounds and high speed by repeated exposure.

Too many sounds of explosions, screaming, exaggerated sound effects of hitting something, even in children's cartoons; the scenes where someone is driving fast and hits an obstacle, all can impact the sense of safety and speed.

Senses of speed and safety can be misled when you play a speed-driving race in video games. The sensory data creates a pattern of thinking that recognizes this high speed as *safe* because after all the bumps and hits on the virtual road, you were safe. Besides, everyone and everything was safe around you after the sound of explosion and screaming.

It all happens at a subconscious level, but you can control it by choosing to play video games or to watch movies that support your safe and healthy responses that protect your life.

No one likes or chooses violence in the real world. But our nervous system is being prepared to accept it through the current art world.

It is best not to choose the subject of violence both as a viewer and as an artist, not to watch or create it in the world of art or literature, even though it's fiction.

What art can do today is to bring realistic hope and realistic possibilities as stories, as music, and in every form of fiction to ease struggle and pain in life.

Story of a Man

A broken man, anxious with the burden of his debt and bills to pay, walks out to the street on a cold winter day to eat a hot meal.

As his debt and bills burden his mind, he passes by a homeless man. The homeless man is curling down in a corner. It breaks his heart to see the man in an even worse situation than he himself is. He wishes he could buy hot food for him too.

The monologue of his rational mind interferes:

"Impossible. There is barely enough for your own meals."

He would usually stop dreaming of the impossible things right away ... But this time, he turns it into a dialogue:

"I feel bad to see him cold and hungry. I know how it feels."

I want to do something.

The rational mind says:

"It's irrational. You must be crazy."

He ponders a while and thinks back:

"Buying him food adds just a bit more to my already heavy debt, instead I would not have to see him weak and cold, which means a lot to me."

It is convincing enough!

He dares to buys two hot meals instead of one, and as he offers it to the homeless man, he becomes rich. Even though a bit more in debt now, he is rich enough not to have to bear with seeing the heart-breaking situation. He was rich enough to change the situation. He will not be having his hot food in the cold where another man starves. His rational mind now suddenly feels rich.

When he managed to change a monologue to a dialogue, art took place in him.

Again when he managed to overcome the mind barrier that was meant to be "rational" but was barely even rational, his point of view in his mind changed, and art happened again.

The rational mind will tend to get back at the old set point again. But the man found the key to turn an irrational monologue to a truly rational dialogue. He found the key to change his perspective into a wiser one.

Art transformed a poor man to a rich man, liberating him from self-pity! That man is living art as long as his brave thinking style surpasses his self-set limits, which is named after rationality, and as long as this transformation still echoes in him.

The art piece is the transformed personality to a more authentic version, a more expansive and more inclusive one so the inner beauty of the man can manifest through it.

The wisest thoughts evolve around love. A work of art is nothing but the birth of an action based on such wisdom; the action that in turn gives birth to a new perspective, a new aspect of who you are. Once you see who you truly are, your mindsets change. Your attitudes change… And your life experiences change.

Chapter III

A Path to Self-Discovery

Melted in what we see around us,
It is hard to find our own pieces between all the others.
So we lose track of who we really are.
So we have to hear from outside our names called.
And what we are named, we will become.
And others, who were named before,
Had named those who named us.
As if we are caught up in a web we ourselves made!
When would we hear our names gently and quietly, called from within?

What is Art Good for?

What is the point of designing a place with colors? How many more of just decorative art pieces that are band aides on deep wounds, blind fold the eyes on the truth inside?

What are paintings good for, what is the point in convincing the mind of 3D vision, while it is in fact an illusion made by a 2D image?

Sometimes none of these work.

We have enough of everything but less of essentials, and the most lost one, is our own Self. The pure self, lost between options of how to be, lost between all labels.

There must be a point, more than just the popularity or the aha moments that art brings to the viewers and listeners. Those aha moments could be created by wonders of nature alone.

There must be a point in doing art, that is not in its physical product, which causes practicing Art continue being a part of human life from stone age to now.

Practicing Art authentically and intrinsically allows love to flow through the mind and heart and leads them ahead. As the sap flowing through the vessels of the plant leads to its growth, flow of love will cause growth and expansion of the mind and heart. This is also how the healing effects of art take place after hurtful events, by re-branching the injured senses and feelings, back to their natural state.

But you won't need an injury to experience its regrowing effects. There is always more room for growth.

Hidden underneath layers of one's own assumptions and the comfort zone they provide, it takes courage, patience and hope, to want to peel the layers off and set them aside. You may hold on to them because that is the only way you know yourself, define yourself and think that without them your reality will not exist anymore.

But your reality will do, and will also shine, when you exist without them.

When you practice art, you practice personal courage, and you acquire patience.

This is the skill required in order to be *You* in life. The you that is lively, lovely and kind.

No one is born bad in nature. If one had made mistakes, bad choices, or gone wrong, it may have been a loop on the road that doesn't lead to anywhere further, but can bring one back to the first place to try again. Mistakes don't come from one's essence and nature.

How to navigate through mazes of life, moments of anger, frustration, flaming emotion, are the skills we need to develop in order to resonate with our own pure self. It is on us to take the sweet or bitter labels off, and live our true self.

Art is the theory and life is the realization of it. But the language in which this theory for life is written has the complexity of language of dreams rather than the language of words used in daily life. That's why it is very important to remove the obstacles that obstruct a two-way communication between you and true art. True art is not in its subject or only about how skillfully it's rendered.

Art is not only an entertainment to occupy your time, or to gift the eyes and ears a short lasting joy, but it is to inspire you with new visions, new ways to go around delicate roads of thoughts and still remain as good as you are.

It really makes a difference in your art if while you develop your art skills and techniques, you manage to keep this authenticity and simplicity in the ways of your thinking at the same time.

The transformation that can happen in the artist's mind during the process of making Art, is far more beautiful than the piece itself.

All forms of art seem to be assigned to all senses, to provide a road map and poetically develop creative solutions in life.

Whether on a piece of paper or in a music piece, the solutions show you new vistas, new ways, without leaving home.

Make sure to get a sense of this dynamic beauty on the face of visual arts, the sound of music or play it in your life as you go.

Practicing Art is the skill to navigate through the unknown, unpredictable. It is the skill that develops by the fuel of love, and later becomes a talent.

Different forms of Art; visual, audio, theatrical, and so on, are in a way, kinds of mediums through which we walk the path of our navigation. Whenever you navigate and explore your way, the piece records it in itself as a map for you and others. An art piece has this capacity to store the indescribable data.

Practicing art in any form holds the footprints of the path the artist's mind had walked, and develops a road map for you and the subconscious mind of the viewer. It keeps an imprint of the emotions and thoughts we go through. Now the data is treasured in a piece of work.

On the way to create an artwork, not only you achieve manual skills but also you develop styles of thinking and unique personal ways of finding solutions. *A few solutions to your problems on canvas may help you solve problems in the actual Art you do in life.* This is because you approach the problems on canvas fearlessly and what you find will be a manner of thinking that opens up a new vision in you. This is why Art still remains a human's life companion even though there has been less public attention on this role of Art for decades.

The big picture of living a life is not a tangible and material form of Art, but it does exist. Designing the big picture of your life artistically is the greatest form of human's art. It is the point where all other arts are initiated. You practice it in Art but the true performance is on the scene of your life.

Art rules become no rules as you practice more. Most art rules are the initial structure to support the beginning. But they become no rules as you branch out your thoughts to new vistas.

The farther you find yourself from hearing the inner voice, the more structure is needed to start the art practice. The closer you are to this voice, like younger kids, the least structure you need to start with.

There is so much to learn from the little artists, but you must not forget that you too were born a little artist someday. Now you are to consciously earn it back since you were distracted from it as you were passing through mazes of life.

Practicing Art walks adults back to the state of being naturally an artist. It reminds you of the place you came from. Through the principles of design, in composition of a music piece or a theatrical scene or simple drawings, Art awakens the memory of the qualities of beauty that resides in hearts, like unity, harmony, anchors of strength and the rhythms.

An unbiased artistic vision, accompanies you on the road to sketch the realities of a landscape with no pre-judgments or assumptions about the light and colors of the sky and the range of the mountains, for they change every moment.

As you learn to see the dynamic beauty that exists around you, you unlearn the fixed habits that cover your true emotions. You become aware of your yearnings and longings.

You walk the path, uncover the self, layer by layer and eventually you are back to your starting point only to see yourself there at the end, but this time with experienced and matured eyes.

You see the beauty that you came here with but forgot about while you were too engaged with the world. Still you engage with the world but this time with opened eyes, aware of the beauty that lies in your truth. This is the marriage of both sides of our existence; the inner and the outer world.

It is what brings the pieces back together. It creates peace inside and emanates love outside.

This is what Art is meant to do for you.

In order to put away the masks that are not yours and the thoughts that are not generated by you, you need to *recognize* them first. Practice your Art in a way that it paves the path for you to meet all those thoughts one by one. Recognize the thoughts that are automatically obstructing your vision of who you really are, by not letting you do what feels right.

Practice listening to your heart and knowing the difference between you heart felt emotions and the external ideas you have adopted.

Art is not only a language of hearts to communicate with each other, but also a language of the heart to communicate with you, showing you the ways and the obstacles, and developing the skills you need in real life, in a compact form. Your heart can speak the deepest secrets to you in your Art if you will. This is the forgotten aspect of Art nowadays.

Many artists focus on creating artwork to connect with the world outside while the inner part of Art's mission is undermined.

So many art students, hoping for the shortest path to destination, follow the path of reproducing copies of master pieces and photographs, forsaking their time and energy by walking around one circle only for so many times. What if they know there is a spiral path with circles that can lead them to higher levels each round. No wonder sometimes the feeling of repetition makes students so bored that from there after, they have to push and struggle emotionally to go on. The path of repetition, is empty from inner rewards of hope and a promise to see the horizon where the sun of their true desire rises. This work can still fill the space of galleries, can win awards but cannot inspire hearts, and does not bring joy to the artist's soul. The joy of social success only blesses the outer shells of persona without touching even the artist's own heart. If we are not in touch with the compass inside, our work may achieve a mere goal that falls short from all what Art could do and was here to accomplish.

Art cannot be enslaved, but it will accompany you anywhere and anytime when your Heart leads your intentions and actions.

You as the Artist

While Art is born of passion and love for beauty and truth, the artist's mind is the instrument through which Art will come to the physical world. The instrument itself is blessed by joy of this mediation.

You may remember the joy you experienced from creating art, be it the kind word you spoke at the right moment or the right brush stroke you put on the right place on your canvas.

Keeping the path of manifestation of art through you clear, supports the purity of your art. The path is the mind. If your art was the kind word you said at the right time, then the purity of your word is protected by clearing the mind from any biased intentions that could have been in the mind at the time, like feeling superiority, expecting an approval and so on.

If intentions of love and simplicity are in the mind at the time of creating art work, they will put an imprint on the artwork. The same is true while creating a piece in music or visual arts. There is an imprint of the artist mind in them. The more simple and clear the artist's mind at the moment of creating, the more pure and authentic the artwork will be.

Even obsessing too much about techniques and skills can affect an artwork with lack of courage and deplete it from liveliness.

Simple, reckless and loving Intentions, with perfect harmony between hands and mind, allow purest kind of Art.

Practicing Art is about practicing pure intentions in an invisible way.

If you are making something with pure and kind intentions, which comes from the deepest source of courage that resides in you, a large part of a true work of Art is done even if you have no experience in doing it. Harmony and balance can find their way into your work naturally when those paths are clear.

The craftsmanship in the way you do art, will develop later by practice, which trains your hands, eyes and mind to create a finer coordination between them.

At times even before this coordination develops between the mind and the body, Art can still appear in the work of someone who has opened lots of ties in their thoughts and mind without spending much time practicing for example drawing. Even with no intentions, their mind, which has become clear and transparent in depth, transmits the light of the love and the life into the piece and turns it to Art.

Art Can Heal Emotions

Emotional healing is simply an emotional growth. Not that subject of healing has been ill before healing, but the subject heals from the wounds of releasing an old skin for the new one that fits. It is healing from the shock of letting go of the familiar good old explanations, definitions and understanding of Self, to the new one that fits and defines the known *self* better. This so called healing is the inner growth, and a beautiful mechanism that detoxifies the reservoir of emotions and makes more room for love. Notice the expressions in free style acting, singing, playing drums ... They all release those unspoken emotions. After this cleansing, comes rest.

The mind at rest notices more loving things around.

A flute is always touched by the air blown into it

Since the mind of human is the passage for Art to be born, not only the artwork has an imprint from the mind of the artist but also the mind and the body of the artist are impressed by the attitude of the piece that is coming to life.

When actors play a scene, they contemplate the scene deeply within as if they live in the realm that they contemplated in their mind. If it's a delightful scene, the joy of living in that contemplated realm can actually delight them in reality.

The artist mind and body can benefit from creating Art. Practicing Art properly can enhance the mind power and increase emotional flexibility to gain back the energy to embrace love again, and to hold it for longer time intervals.

When the play imitates a sad event, it also affects the artist and the viewer. As the artist imagines the realm of the act or play, it feels real to the inner senses and the senses will respond. If it is imagining a violent speed, the senses will adapt to it. Sometimes when a sad story is imagined and played, the actors should retreat after the play for their senses to come back to the usual state of mind. The actors who play speed driving need to take some time to re-adjust the sense of speed and safety in their actual daily driving. Still the problem will remain for the faithful observer of the show that keeps on watching the speed driving movies and games. It matters to make a choice in which realm we are contemplating or intending to bring into the artwork. Whether the realm is violent or peaceful, portraying frustration or hope, the artist who holds the realm in mind, will be affected or benefit from it.

Chapter IV

The Practice of Art

A Way of Thinking

Flying Bird

Imagine a bird flying in the sky, moving its wings, cutting through the air every second to keep its body up at the height of its desire in the sky. It is a flying bird.

When it reaches the height it desired, it lands on a mountain. It now becomes a resting bird. A seated bird.

The bird can rest and it can nest, but to be a flying bird again, it shall listen to the call, fall in love with the sky, leave the nest behind and fly again. Taking the risk of flying to the unknown mountains, facing the danger of becoming a prey, or at least losing a settled resting place on the top, is the deal.

No matter how far it has flown so far, no matter how long and how well its wings have performed the flights in the past, they cannot make a seated bird, a flying one. They can only be good companions to the bird's desire to fly. And the desire is what makes the bird a Flying Bird. The joy for a bird is ultimately to fly and not become an ever-seated bird on top of a mountain. Sitting is not the bird's calling. An ever-seated bird in the nest on the top, has the safety and security that is also found in a cage.

Becoming an Artist Everyday

You become an Artist first, then you create your work of Art. Art is born from the source of your being. It appears in the mind before it appears in the work of Art. You must acknowledge it internally before you can perform it.

To become an artist, awareness of passage of moments or passage of time is needed. Every morning you gain new courage to fall in love with life, and art will be born in you. Artistic power cannot be hoarded somewhere in time. It can't accumulate just as time cannot be accumulated. You may become an artist every morning when you wake up from sleep. Everyday there's a glimpse of love and life pulse that you can catch from morning to night till you go to sleep. Then you let it go and rest. Tomorrow when you wake up you get another fresh chance to fall in love again and become an artist. When you take the chance, you are an artist, again. It's an everyday happening process. Starting all over fresh and new.

Never get stuck in your own creativity from your past achievements. Never follow your own created art patterns and styles that have no pulse anymore. When you truly like the past patterns, if you let them go, you will find yourself falling in love with them the next day, only this time without fear of losing them.

In some seasons, whether it's a season of the year, or a season of thoughts, the mind is more fertile, you are more ready to fall in love with the energy of life and will be more active in becoming the artist every day.

Some other times feels like a winter, the passion is still there but resting, as it's gaining new potentials. That's when you see yourself drawn into daily issues, with least signs of vitality in your creativity, and all that's left in your work, your practice of art, is the same style of work you used to do before, only with no pulse.

Don't challenge yourself in those times. Don't blame yourself and don't promise anyone that you will do a masterpiece for them in those times. Your daily distractions, adventures, experiences, problems regardless of pain and pleasure they bring you, are there to feed the soil where your seeds of passion are sleeping. At the right season the seeds will start to rise from the ground of your being, no matter how busy you still are! Just remember to allow them some room once they start to grow even if they seem too unfamiliar and irrelevant.

Worrying over Consistency

The concept of consistency and integrity in a body of artwork causes a conclusion, that you must persist in your ideas, all your paintings can only be integrated around the same theme and same style, and therefore you have to hold onto your viewpoints!

Let it be intermittent instead of constant! Let the fresh flow of life spread around your ideas and bless them with vitality. Your creative ideas, if tuned with this live pulsation, will grow back, here and there, in various themes and styles, but around one thread. And a chain of artwork will form itself, just like your vision that expands and grows with them.

Worrying over consistency of creative ideas or doing art the way you feel like today, shouldn't be the artist's dilemma. Consistency and integration takes place when you hold on to *your truth* as you work on any subject or any theme.

Maybe consistency is about insisting on leaving enough space for this flow, and maybe integrity is about the integrated connection of all of your senses to the breath of life that's pulsing in you and around you. That is your integrity; the connection to who you are, the *true you* that creates the work of art. The rest is fiction.

The Unspoken Language

Knowing the true language of your heart is the key. You can call this language of the subconscious mind. It is a shared language between living things. Even the flowers know the sky, and the stones hold on to the warmth of a loving touch. But the language also retains the impressions of the individual life that you have lived so far in it, as well. You have felt joy, or felt fear or anger and your personal, symbolic language was formed through those experiments. Hints from those signs and symbols ignite feelings of joy, fear or anger in your communications with the world. Personal memory creates a virtual reality around you that is like a translucent layer. As it lets the images in, it also *displays* its own design if it has any, on the image of the realities you see from the world.

It has been a medium between you, the world around you, and the world within you. It is the same language that has spoken to you in your dreams. It is also the *Filter* between you and both worlds inside and out. You can familiarize yourself with the deepest language of your heart, or on the surface where language has been formed through your life experiences, you can find misconceptions, cleanse it and help it refresh and become transparent so you can see the world inside and outside through it better.

Practicing art *actively* and *consciously*, helps you find a new discipline of thinking of your own, by which the seemingly random things can relate and make new sense and reveal their meaning. You practice in music, painting ... and the strength you build up in your harmonic thinking, will be beneficial in creating a meaning, a new sense in the area of your efforts, challenges and joy in life.

In the beginning of art practice, there may be a strong tendency towards a specific color, for some sort of composition, a type of music or sound or fashion, that may feel unreasonable but you long to give in to it as much as you fear to put it on your canvas, or in your music or your style. There is a meaning in your longing. You do not fight it, but learn to recognize it, witness it silently and let it show up in your work, without expecting your work to become a hit, your fashion style to be approved, your Art to bring you success. You do not have to even show it to anyone. You do not have to stick to this style forever. Maybe it is there only to communicate with you, to tell you a secret about yourself that has not formed words yet. So listen with the patience and acceptance that you listen to a child. The language of subconscious mind is mild and kind. It is symbolic and the symbolism matches your personal vocabulary, the visual or sound memory vocabulary that has developed during your life experience.

At this point of practice, not interfering with the expression of your subconscious mind brings you closer to your mind qualities, makes you even aware of the unknown in your life. How much fear you have stored, how much bravery you have supplied yourself with, what are those suppressed emotions you never dared to express to yourself, in fear of being judged by you! Listen to all you hear without deciding if it is right or wrong. This is your kingdom, and your safe place. So keep it private and confidential and let your inner feelings show up in your visual or music or kinetic language when you do art, allow yourself to hum, dance or speak, and clear up the path to your *true self* as it washes away the stored emotions and also gives you a record of what has been going on so far.

The practice, applies to all forms of art. I will explain it in visual arts since it's the form of art I've mainly practiced.

Sitting in front of a blank canvas

Once you are sitting in front of a blank canvas or paper, and you feel doubtful about where to start, how to start, scared from the possible mistakes, and have every tool for erasing it ready, allow me a moment, that's when I wish to speak to you.

If it is an assignment or if it is a personal decision, remember, *You* as the one sitting in front of that blank canvas calling for images, own it. You have a choice of not doing it at all if you feel pressured.

If you decide to do it, still the canvas is also the kingdom of your choices. Do it the way your heart says, the way that makes sense to your heart. Time for art is not time to follow rules derived from art. Time for art, is time to experiment art, to examine ideas, to exercise thinking.

If you are doing art and you are getting more stressed, then consider that your meter indicates there is a pressure on you! There may be a demand or call for you that is not a call from *Art*. It may be the collective habit of thinking that surrounds you.

Take a deep breath and quit practicing right there ... This path would not take you to art.

You'll find your way to be stress free, from the very beginning. Start fresh with a new perspective on practicing art.

When you are in front of a blank paper, let your mind also be as clear as the blank paper, wiped off of the expectations of other people's minds that are adopted by yours.

Let the silence ignite a dialog between *you* and *you*, in front of the canvas.

Promise yourself that you will support and protect whatever

expression shows up on your paper or canvas by your inner feelings.

Protect it from the gestures of those who have not yet known all possibilities of what may happen on a canvas. Stay on this promise like a true friend does.

Do not also replay the words and expectations of others constantly, and if it would still play automatically, just hear it and do not put your attention on it. Do what you have planned, the simplest lines will do.

Inner Dialog

As you work, you listen and keep listening wholeheartedly to your inner talks.
At first you hear more of the talks about *dos* and *don'ts.*
Listen, but only listen.
Listen like a silent witness.
Do not judge, do not fight.
Do not rebel against your mind dialogs.
They will subside. Just listen to them kindly and let them pour out as you stay on what you had planned to do.
Let them subside.
You know now what is the first stage!
It is a scene of controversy of all ideas that your mind has been exposed to and has acquired.
These ideas have nothing to do with creativity even though they command you to do your art this way or that way.
All they have to do is with the fear of failure, disapproval by yourself or others.

Your self-talk appears in episodes. After what you hear from adopted ideas that command you to do it this way or that way is cleared, The inner feelings show up. They might be complains or expressions of how you dislike what you do, or how you feel about your paintings or so on. Listen to them and respect them ...

Joyful feelings also come. Respect them too. As your hands are moving along the canvas, these thoughts or feelings may seem irrelevant and have nothing to do with what you are doing, but in fact, their live movements are flowing into your work. They leave some trace from themselves along the lines and the structure of your work.

Letting them be expressed without judging or stopping them, keeps your work pure and honest.

Please do not obstruct their flow. They have an episode and will be gone if they find an outlet.

Later, when you learn how to embrace every wave of thoughts, and when the pressure of accumulated ones from the past has reduced, what is left to be expressed is only the dilemmas of the Now. You are at this stage in tune with *present time*, where creativity takes a major turn. As you tuned inside, your creativity was an outlet to reveal acquired thoughts and later to express your unspoken personal pain and pleasure from the past.

Now after a while of practicing in this way, you have a clearer path of thinking while you do art, and you have a view on the outer and inner world with no blurry vision that the accumulated feelings could cause. With the better vision, you can manage life problems better. Your artwork also becomes more keen and powerful.

As you keep on embracing the reality of your feelings, gradually non-personal inspirations will flow through your mind. With your clear and honest thinking style, your mind becomes a place for the pure flow of life that finds its way then into your work.

As you keep steering well for so long, sometimes, something

beyond the flowing paint takes care of your intentional painting. The paint may happen to create a sense of the moonlight on the leaves while you were on a promise not to fight anything that shows up.

Something you didn't even think you could do because it was complicated, but it happened, as you persisted on your commitment.

This live energy will keep on brushing your other paintings as you keep on staying in a balanced, quiet and kind mode to what happens on your canvas.

As you purify your mind, spontaneity shifts from being impulsive or even compulsive, to a kind response to demands of the present moment ...

And the path gradually becomes clear. Beauty can be sensed through these paths. You can probe for beauty through the doorways of all your senses. In this way of practice, the sense that you use the most, expands and becomes more sensitive to beauty. Visual artists develop their vision of beauty, musicians develop the power of listening to beauty and the vocalist sings the beauty, on a stream of notes and words.

Noticing the self-talk and not listening to it may be risky in life situations. We cannot be sure yet if it is coming from a place of fear or wisdom. Do they warn us of real danger or false one?

But in art practice you can proceed to test them and examine your self-talks without any risk or harm in real life. What happens, happens only on your canvas. Listening and even choosing to do the opposite of what you hear, can't be harmful on your canvas. This is a safe realm that practice of art provides you, to turn every where you want and develop your sense of courage, expand your point of view, have an overall view on your own thoughts and experimenting the *otherwise*, without ruining real life situations. This is the place for it.

What happens if the lines I draw are not drawn the way I think they should be? Will it mess up my painting? Let's see if it really does!

At times you will see that they do not mess up your painting at all.

Opening up to oneself might be the scariest part of practice. The fear of letting go that can cause a flood ... of course we tend to prevent it, or obstruct it.

It is the fear that arises when an art practitioner is in front of a blank page or a musician at the silence of the audience before the start.

Everything is inviting you to flow but the fear haunts! Do it your way. There is no guaranty if you do it according to the *dos* and *don'ts* you will be happier.

The flood of energy that you fear from is not destructive. It is constructive. It is the power that eventually constructs the basis of your art and performance. It is true with your life as well in case you choose to practice art directly in your life not on a canvas or your music!

Your true creative work is to navigate through the mind's pathways while practicing art, without getting stuck. Reaching the end of a half an hour timeframe you had set up for yourself to draw and paint in a *gentle thinking style,* is an achievement, even if you only painted a square in red.

Practice drawing a square and paint it red

Draw the lines but don't use a ruler. Simply your hand can lead your pen to the right place.

And the pen can be enough for your hand to lean on. Don't lean your hand on the paper and just lean on the tip of your pen. Your square might be dancing on the paper but it's fine.

Keep on drawing as you listen for the self-talks. You may percept them in form of feelings as if you have messed up, or it has no use to practice such simple shape, or as if it's going to be a masterpiece.

Just keep going.

When you are done with the square, look at your square not as a shape but as the formation of lines that have changed direction a few times. How are the lines doing? They are carrying your feelings of the moment in them.

Now paint your square in red, or ... say no to my suggestion and instead see what your heart feels like ... Painting inside or not painting at all? Paint it in red? Who knows but you? ...

Everyone has a personal kind of talent. What is hard to do is to dare to see it, to dare to cultivate it. It feels risky because it is not a discovered and paved path yet. *You* are the one who can pave it. That is probably why a lot of talented people tend to follow the work style of another talented person who's been proven successful. The successful artist's path was already tested in good results. The true art is to dare leave this path leading to the expected results, knowing it is possible to pave another path to better results. I think the art work that can be made by potential artists will be as great as those achieved by proven successful artists. If Art is the language of the soul and each soul has something good to say or share, then who knows better than you, what your soul wants to share?

First thing you need to know about art, is how to tune with your soul.

Each one of us carries a *jewel* that is hidden inside.

Doing art is a journey full of life lessons. The journey in art has in it a version of life puzzles and games that are unique to your life, yet a core structure that is in common with everyone.

Putting pieces together in a meaningful way, even as an art practice requires alertness, calmness and thoughtfulness.

It would be a waste to spend time practicing with such great master, and get distracted from learning what it teaches by looking the other way on the physical product of the practice.

The invaluable product of art is the transformation that happens in you. When you encounter the same old situation but you respond in a thoughtful new way, you have created a new pathway of thinking, a new way of connection between areas of brain, which designs the tapestry of you presence in the world where your true self can manifest!

Rulers and erasers seem quite unnecessary while drawing! Not having them around will leave those ways open for you to practice and develop the neuromuscular connections needed to keep your hands in tune with what you desire to draw. There is no mistake and there is nothing wrong with a few shivering lines at first. As you practice you develop these pathways, and the lines you draw become steadier!

Also by putting the erasers aside, you practice your courage for taking risks on the surface of a canvas where it doesn't hurt you or anyone.

Reproducing copies

What a world it will be when it is filled with paintings that are copies of one another! Lots of paintings from pictures, all 2D copies of another 2D painting or photo origin!

The world is 3 Dimensional; its image that falls on the retina of the eyes is 2Dimensional. The 2D image is interpreted as the 3D again after optical area of brain processes it.
What we understand from the 2D image is a 3 dimensional world.

The visual artist's mind is trained to also walk back the path from the 3D perception to a 2D, and design the lines and colors on a flat surface of canvas in a way that creates an illusion of a three dimensional space. When you look at a beautiful painting, a photo of scenery, or a portrait painting that feels alive, you are looking at fiction. It's a two dimensional object that can create the illusion of a three dimensional reality.

This is the magic that takes place in the artist's mind. Does this magic happen when painting from a 2D image like a photo or another painting, and reproducing another 2D image again?... Then why even bother?

We must have missed the point.

We no longer need to think through a way to carry water and store it in our homes. Many of daily problems in life have been solved through creative inventions of human before us.

The paths have been paved outside. What we need to do is to pave inner paths of our mind.

If we tend to follow templates even in artistic activities, then our creativity will have no place in our mind.

I hope we can free ourselves from making copies and using already made patterns at least when we paint, we dance or write ...

Things to remember before you practice

There is no specific way your art should look like. It is more about the specific way of being *you* while doing art. Keep your mind pure by staying free from following any styles, or even free from intentions in earlier levels of practice. Once you master the skill of keeping your mind clear and free during practice, pure intentions that generate unique beauty of their kind will come to your work.

It is important to be comfortable with yourself as you practice art. Accept yourself the way you are, know that you are moving forward anyway. Be honest with yourself, open up to yourself and listen.

Being gentle is the key to your progress. Never expand an understanding of a situation, by recreational drugs or excessive practice. In order to expand the range of motion in a stiff joint, it should not be numbed and then forced to expand. It causes a damage that brings back the stiffness again later.

Creativity cannot be forced into action, however it cannot be stopped either.

Instruments, Tools and Mediums

Artists are in love not only with beauty but as a consequence they also love their instruments, tools and mediums for creating their artwork.

Artists care a lot about their tools and instruments, never neglecting them. They condition their tools for more longevity, be it a paintbrush or the strings of a violin. As the artist that you are, you must always take care of what makes creation of your art possible.

Your Body and Mind

Your body and mind are the first and foremost instruments you need for doing your art. We often forget that our most important anchor for creating any kind of art is our body, our mind and the relation between them known as the neuromuscular pathways. Neuromuscular pathways provide the finest movements in body synchronized to what's heard or sensed internally, harmonizing motions with your feelings when you draw and with the music when you dance.

Make sure you don't compromise your physical being in process of producing art. When you are going to work long hours with full passion for creating, meet your body's needs first. Put your body and mind before any of your instruments and your brushes. Keep them sharp and condition them by good sleep, healthy food and fresh air. Keep your body in a good posture and your mind, transparent and free of illusions. There is a relation between the two.

The cleaner the atmosphere of your mind is, the better you get the waves of inspiration and the easier you relay them.

Conditioning your most important tools

Imagine how long it takes you to practice and master the techniques you wish to learn. Then imagine how long you would like to continue experimenting the art you have mastered. It can be a lifetime! You would want to condition and take care of your body and support it from negative effects of long hours of sitting or standing for this practice, so you can still keep on working your art for years to come. When you master your area of work, you still deserve to work with joy, not with pain.

Well positioning the body and mind

Once you are ready for creating a piece, what is needed is a good position for the body and good atmosphere in thoughts. What we do in art practice after exploration is expanding and exercising the mind. Our mind and body work so hand in hand that providing a fluent energy for the body empowers the mind. Keeping the body in the best possible posture; the closest body position to the default postural structure, helps you think and focus better.

Develop the physical aspect of your art, by providing the body with power, enough endurance for long hours of practice and a healthy posture for the years of practice to come.

Why does a good posture help energy better flow through the body?

Every muscle fiber that naturally contracts has received some impulse from the brain through neurons that innervate it. When you keep a good posture, all the muscles that are responsible for keeping your position in relation to gravity are at work.

A good posture is a balanced and firm position in sitting, standing, walking and so on, for your body and organs to function their best. It is naturally and uniquely designed for each person, but much similar in all. Good posture can also be achieved while adopting assistive device.

Holding a good posture requires work of muscles. Once each neuron fires a level of electricity, a mild contraction is created in each muscle fiber, the sum of which provides the force to keep the body upward, against but in line with gravity. As long as they hold the body up, this electric pulse keeps leaping through the neuron extensions, called axons, to the destination in muscles. How well organized they work together matters.

According to the laws of physics, a moving electric charge induces a magnetic field. Imagine, in a see-through model, the axons and the charges traveling through them, originating from the brain to various destinations in muscles, like strings of light that create a bright field around themselves. Many of those lights turn on with a good posture where designated groups of muscles, prepared for the job, work. The beams are aligned and add up. In a loose posture though, less lights are on for less muscles work, most of which aren't even designated for the job, and ligaments and joints bear with the rest of the body's weight. As each segment has a different direction from other segments, the field of light along the strings seems scattered, diffused and dimmed. With a good posture, the body's economy of magnetic energy is bountiful, and so will benefit the mind.

We all know our best posture possible. You can feel better and function your best if you add your best possible posture to the good work you do. If you align your body with the default posture designed for your daily activity by nature, or the nearest possible posture to that, you will benefit from this harmonized flow of energy created by your body to bring out the best in you.

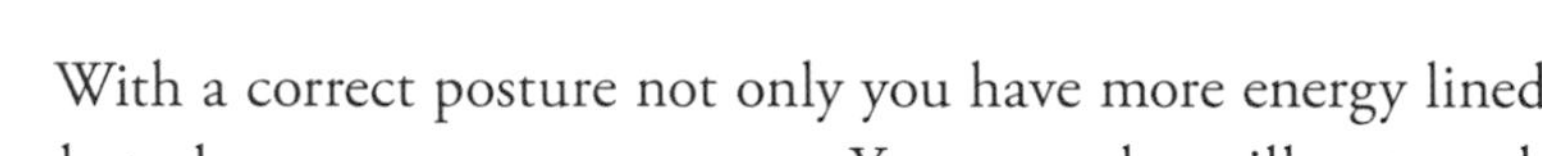

With a correct posture not only you have more energy lined up, but also you save your energy. Your muscles will not work too hard.

When the body is not completely aligned with the line of gravity, like in bending forward to reach something, in order to hold the body against gravity and prevent falling, more work is expected from the postural muscles. Also other muscles must join to get the work done. If bending forward, or sideways becomes a position you always do your art in, it will not only make the postural muscles tired, but also will engage the muscles that are not prepared with the endurance necessary for this kind of work.

This can cause tension and muscle pain that appears after you finish your work for the day. I think it's the worst sneaky obstacle on the way of practicing art that can disappoint you from continuing. The body will remember the pain from the previous sessions and you will somehow feel reluctant for practice even though you love to do art!

Make sure at the end of a session, not to stretch tense muscles around the neck, shoulder and spine. They are very fine muscles and little stretching can hurt them if they are still tense after work. Pay attention to them during the session, and after the session is done, if they are still tense, just rest and let them open up at their own pace.

Posture becomes a habit

Thinking of the long run, the position you put your body in, tends to form a habit for your muscles. It is very important to sit in a balanced position as you practice. Allowing a misaligned posture like leaning sideways to become a habit, puts the muscles of one side in a position shorter than usual, and the opposite side in a longer length, more often. The stretched muscles will be in a relaxed mode and gradually adapt to less work. On the bent side, the muscles will adapt to their new shorter length as their new normal. After years, the tiny joints around the spine will have to adapt to theses little changes as well. A lifetime of practice without noticing these changes and appropriate exercise can bring some inflexibility in the misaligned posture. The fixated misalignment is still reversible under supervision and help of the health care professionals.

It has happened gradually through a habit of bad posture, so it may gradually reverse, by changing the habit. But what a long way to go when you can easily prevent it in the first place.

Keeping up with the best posture possible, forms a habit that is a priceless investment for future.

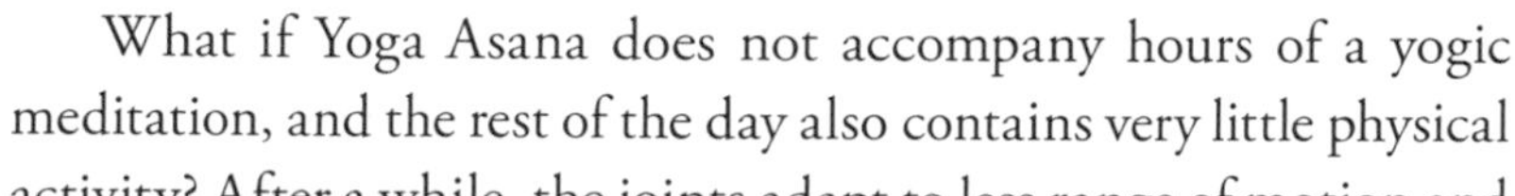

What if Yoga Asana does not accompany hours of a yogic meditation, and the rest of the day also contains very little physical activity? After a while, the joints adapt to less range of motion and muscles that are not used very often, reduce their mass.

In fact, the adverse effects of long hours of sitting aren't only because of working behind the desk. Even sitting well-aligned and flexibly in a cross-legged position to meditate for hours could bring knee weakness after years if the routine didn't include gentle exercise, stretching and walks to balance the practice. (Walking can be both exercise and a modified meditation practice—meditating while walking—that can contribute to the balance of both mind and body).

If the mind develops, and the body development is forgotten, the journey cannot start; like an airplane's flight that can't start if only the side of the pilot's cabin picks up from the ground and the rest of the airplane doesn't.

Harmonic maturation

Your mind, your body, and your heart fly together. When you engage in thoughts or actions that make you lighter in mind and healthier in the body, your heart can pull up and they all rise higher! You would not need anything else! Your equipments for your happiness are all built in. Your conscious work of art is to take care of the health and clear function of this system and not lean on another system to pull you up.

It will make sense if every art session will start with minutes of a gentle exercise and follow in every break until the end of the session.

The language of the mind is also based on a sense of gravity, and space. The language of mind senses progress as a direction of movement, reads responsibilities as heavy loads and relief as lightness. The mind speaks the same language to the body; having too much responsibility feels like carrying weight on the back, and the body takes a bent forward posture with round shoulders as if it is bearing weight. The mind language in visual arts, associates colors, lines and shapes with weight, lightness and movement in between. Feeling a sense of balance in a painting comes from that sense of gravity.

You can speak to your mind, through the colors, lines, shapes that you choose for your space (like in Interior design) and through your body posture as well. But make sure this message is always honest and well meaning, not misleading you from your way of getting to your truth.

Mind Purifying Effects of Art practice

There are times you do art in order to calm the mind through the meditative quality of art making. There are also times that you first meditate and free your mind from any worries and then you do art.

The way to get to this meditative art passes through the first type of practice. You first learn how to do art to bring calmness to yourself, recognize and free your mind from the obstructive dialogs and demand. Then gradually you will find the vessel of the mind clean and empty, ready to be filled with the reflections of the beauty in the universe, while doing art.

The second way of doing art transfers the peacefulness and the wisdom of those tranquil moments to the viewers and the atmosphere around where the work is displayed.

Your state of mind permeates in to any work you do.

Mind cleansing takes place in several steps. In each step, deeper layers are unveiled.

As much as singing and dancing to your own songs relaxes you, *Drawing long lines* on newsprints or paper that is going to be recycled, with no specific subject to sketch from, can physically release emotions that are hard to put in words. The release happens through the movements of the arm as you draw on paper. It frees your mind from the first layer of worries.

Cleansing and freeing your mind from worries and mindsets that interrupt your ways of thinking, not only is a step forward on your way of self-discovery, but also will bring the purity and invites best intentions into your work as well.

It may not be possible to expect your good intentions to flow into your work with no barriers in the beginning. Therefore, practice releasing emotions for a long time.

Through an in depth practice of art, your mind becomes an instrument for the voice of nature and depth of your heart.

When you reach the point that you are in touch with the deepest wisdom in you, your art belongs to all. Then practicing the postural balance is the least thing that must be done but an important one.

The physical balance contributes to the mind balance.

As you do your work, your state of mind permeates to what you do or make and transfers to your viewers and listeners any way.

Your physical balance, and your mind dialogs bring you to a state of mind that can better host good intentions like kindness and peace.

The state of mind you achieve in physically balancing your posture has an imprint on your work.

As a committed artist to spread the good in you everywhere, you not only work with good intentions of love and beauty, but also treat yourself and your body in a balanced loving way.

When you position yourself in a *well aligned body posture,* when you *breathe in slowly and deeply* and you are *calm and freed in mind*, your loving intentions flourish and bring in to this world the art that is the best of yours. This best of your art, will upgrade each day as you practice in this mode, and the only standard for comparison is your work in the past.

Producing art happens and flows through your being

When you engage in an act of love and compassion like charity work and so on, you become a medium, an instrument.

The love that heals, comes from the source and passes through your persona and your physical being, and then reaches others.

If love brings light, then it illuminates you first. If love heals, then the artist in love will be first one who will benefit from wellbeing. This is not the labor of love, but a feast of love.

As you do art, you put your persona and your body in touch with realms related to the subjects of your creativity. If It is drama, a story of love or violence, the realm you contemplate, passes through you to become part of the physical world.

Violent or emotionally traumatic art is a trend in entertainment now. Make sure you have a good and loving reason for your beautiful heart, if you chose to play or write a violent scene due to job responsibilities. The intentions that motivated you to make the choice are your support. Coming from a place of love, those intentions can make the process of bringing the creative work or production softer and less corrosive to your own body and mind. But intentions lower than love may not be worth it going through this corrosive process.

As mentioned in chapter III, artists tune with their subjects in order to get a deep feeling of the persona they are going to play, subject they are going to write about or paintings they are commissioned to do. This lets their mind body and soul take a tour in that realm and familiarize with it, as if they adopt another personal life in them. If this realm somehow relates to love and compassion, passing through the instrument of their body and mind, it reflects itself in the artist's mind for quite a while if not for long. If the realm is fear, or sadness it will also do the same. Art is a media, as well as the artist who becomes a medium between the two realms of imagination and the physical. The artist bears the flow of creativity that will cross along, and the first one to be in touch with the imagined realm.

It matters to choose the realm of your imagination wisely and based on clear vision and pure intentions. Sometimes it costs more in the long run, to choose to work in a way which only sells better and attracts more attention, rather than working on what comes from the place of love in your heart.

Eventually what comes from the place of love in your heart, will find its place again in the hearts.

Drawings and Paintings of the Outer Reality

Learning to draw from *reality* resembles learning to *research* in science. Then it moves on to learning to draw from *inner realities* (not inner illusions), making drawings and paintings, which are like *inventions* in science.

An art practitioner surpasses his or her mindsets about realities, and probes for what is, at this moment and beyond assumptions.

Practicing drawing from reality is noting down what's in the outer world by sketching. It's our way of interpretation from the physical world outside.

Why Practice Drawing and Painting from Still Life?

To see the direction and angles of the lines that meet to form the shape of a pot, to see the effects of the shade on the color of the pot, to forget previous assumptions about the shape and color of pots, flowers, and so on, and adhering to the way it seems now under the light projected on them, all teach and train the mind to focus on what is, not what was. It helps avoiding the auto play of thoughts that program our mind in daily life, by practicing a mindful, realistic observance of everything.

Drawing and Paintings of the Inner Realities

But what are the techniques to express our non-physical world, our emotions and thoughts? How do you picture happiness?

Do you do it using images of subjects that bring happiness? Like a field full of tulips? Then what is in the grass field or the flowers or the sky, that gives you a sense of happiness? Is it the abundance? Or a sense of love?

Here you step in the art language when you gradually find that it's not only reds of the flowers in the field that give you the joyful emotion but the minimal surface of reds, the red dots, in the midst of the vast surface of less intense colors in green, where none of these colors and shapes alone could be a sign for happiness. Their presence side by side at this exact size and degree of intensity is what makes the feeling of joy arise. The language is a hidden language that's found in the relationships and the ratios, not the subjects of paintings! Find the right colors, right ratio between their intensity and sizes, and arrange them together without intending to paint scenery and still feel the same sense of abundance and joy. It will be an abstract painting. Now only a touch of gray in a corner, can remind you of a cottage and the painting tends to point towards realism. Knowing the right color and right ratio are the secret, and there's a clue in your heart what they are.

And this story was only about the colors, but other elements do have their story and play their part as well. The lines and dots there can create illusion of colors, weight, movement, directions and texture. The shapes also create a sense of energy in the painting. Their energy seems like magnetism in a two dimensional visual world!

Our mind interprets the inner world based on its in-depth language.

The nervous system has an ability to recognize an object by the touch, called *Stereognosis.*

Through touch, brain can visualize a model of what it has not seen. This ability is explained through an example, when you have your eyes closed and an eraser is put in the palm of your hand without telling you what it is, by sensing the weight and the size and texture of it, you can tell it's an eraser. There are ways for us to tell what we don't see, by its characteristics, sound, taste or smell, through hearing, tasting, and etc.

I think this ability in a reverse mode, is responsible for conveying the visualizations to various characters and spatial view until the visualizations make their way into an art form.

I believe this route of perception is the link between our imagination and actualizing it in art.

Imagine a sculptor who forms clay with closed eyes. Sculptors shape clay with a touch of their hands and finger tips, and convey the existing 3D visualization in mind to clay.

I encourage my students before drawing from still life, not only to turn around the still life arrangement to see it from various angles, but also to hold the objects, like the apple, leafs, or the geometric volumes, in their hands with closed eyes and sense it, weigh it, hear the sound it can make, and understand it at a deeper sensory level. This practice brings their focus of all senses together and inwards, and later in doing art from inner realities, it helps them better contemplate and perform their inner feelings or imaginations.

As mentioned in chapter I, seeing is an integrated way of perception through all other senses as a network of many neurons not only optic nerve. The beauty of this integration is that once art is conceived, it manifests through all these sensory channels. Everyone has a vision of the beauty, like a personal gate to this realm. Everyone has a way of expression of beauty as well. It happens somewhere beyond brain cells. The realm in which it happens is still a mystery.

Drawing from Reality is the Beginning Level of Meditation

Practicing few minutes of silence as opposed to thinking, listening as opposed speaking, seeing as opposed to projecting, and sensing by reception as opposed to searching for something to sense. These are good ways to have better concentration and to enhance external sensory levels of mind, which are the doors into inner realities as well. How you will seem from outside, is a seated silent person as if you are in deep meditation, while you are in fact concentrating on external pathways of your senses. One step at a time!

Practicing to see instead of projecting our own mindset on the objects is the first thing we do in drawing and painting exercise. It resembles the principles of research in terms of having an unbiased view in the process of searching. This means we do not mix our assumptions with what really is seen from the subject of work.

When you practice drawing from realities, to improve your drawing skills, do not identify your subject; identifying, would be your mind set interfering with seeing the model! It is a kind of judgment.

This practice is done through a similar but a parallel route to recognizing the eraser in hand when eyes are closed. In that situation, recognition is done using the mind set, a previous knowledge. Here in drawing from reality, we do not aim to recognize but we want to see it, without putting a name or meaning for it. So forget your knowledge about the subject of drawing; a cup, an apple… and see it like you have never seen it before. If that's hard, you can turn it backwards, or upside down to make it easier for you to get passed by pre definitions that interfere with your mind in process of seeing. Turn around it, watch it with a fresh mind, and evaluate it by the heart, the ratios of width to length, depth and the texture. Let what is in the moment sit and register in your mind, not a repetition of prior definitions. Later as you proceed in practicing, allow your mind develop music or a rhythm from what you draw. By then you have learned to tune with the model, and what a joy you get just in drawing a tiny leaf.

Let the rhythms of your heart beat count the branches on the trees, let it keep track of the beats in songs you play. Have deep feelings instead of numbers. Let yourself sense the quantities by quality of your feelings.

Drawing/Painting Practice to Refresh and Restart Your Vision

The games are individual exercises. They should be done in separate sessions. Each game needs a couple of weeks to settle, so proceed to the next one after two weeks. Each game opens the way for the next one so practice them in the order suggested.

Practice each game as often as you want during the course of two weeks, everyday or couple times a week.

During the weeks of practice, put the drawings or paintings you do, somewhere you can see very often during the day. They are not for sharing yet, they are very personal at this time.

There will be no mistakes in your drawing and painting in this game. So put away all tools for erasing.

Game 1: Paint your canvas all in one color and then start drawings on your colored canvas.
Painting your canvas has an emotional release effect, and you can start hearing your self-talks even before you start drawing.
Still, if for some reason painting the surface of the canvas is not possible for you at the time, colored paper or cardboards will work the same for the rest of the practice.
Paint the surface of your canvas with the color of your choice.
Draw a subject of your choice as well, if you want, even draw with no subjects, just do it your way.
Use pen, pencil, brush and paint, or any tools and mediums you are comfortable with. Make sure your subject is also simple and you are comfortable drawing it. If new to drawing, choose a subject that can be simplified into only one geometrical shape not few. Like an apple instead of cluster of grapes.
Each time you practice, allow yourself to change any of the choices you made, but stick to the essential practice; drawing on any colored canvas or paper, and better if you color it yourself.

Game 2: plan to do a simple painting but paint with exactly the colors you think you should not; the color you usually used to avoid or thought is not suitable.
Listen to your feelings and inner dialog as you paint, but don't follow the command at this time, just practice as mentioned above and study your feeling on the side.

Game 3: draw objects from an angle you have never drawn before like from the top view. Put the plate of fruits on the ground and study drawing them as you are standing up. Put the apple on the top shelf and study it from the viewpoint below the subject.

Game 4: Look deeply at a model of your choice then put the model aside and draw only from what remained in your memory, without looking back.
If it was the apple you studied in different angles several times in previous week, then just draw it from memory without looking at it.
But do choose something new too. Something a little bit more complex.

Game 5: Draw objects symmetrical to how you see them. A mirror image of them.
As you keep on looking deep into your model, for example a small pot of a live plant, draw the outlines of the subject you see on the right, on the left side and vice versa. Try to keep your eyes mostly on the model as you draw. During the time you draw, just check your drawing only a few times.

The first three games are to change the limitations that we consider necessary so we never exceed beyond them.

The fourth and fifth game, exercise the visual memory, and concentration. ...

When practicing drawing, pay attention to your model; look at it for some time, calmly. Watch, in a silent mind to understand the model with clear vision.

You will draw lines with more conviction and better composition if you know your subject well, if you know it the way it is, not the way you assume it to be. This is also how you start your path to self-discovery. You start from what is seen outside and you work your way to a deep presence in the moment, where the *true you* resides.

Self-portrait

Practicing self-portraits using a mirror is a way to know more about the mindsets we have about ourselves.

When doing a self-portrait from a mirror, what is seen from the out side is the persona, a shell, a mask. The persona may have done rights or wrongs, and may not have earned your approval. You will face your hidden personal judgments as you gaze at your image in the mirror to draw it. As you know how to listen but not yield to the first layer of complains in self-talks, ignore any mind comments on your persona and your look, just watch what you see in your silent mind. What you see from yourself in a mirror, regardless of how you like it or not, is not the real you anyway!

The path of self-discovery requires letting go of mindsets about yourself so that blame, hatred and fear will not find its way to your thoughts, and you become a friend, first to this image.

Before you can express your deepest intents in art, you must open this door in order to enter; knowing what your mind has projected on your own reality, awareness of the illusions about the image.

You get past this door by seeing what stands between your awareness and the real You.

Practicing art is more of a mind practice rather than just hand eye coordination skill. It is the power of cognitive thinking that advances to a level of pure vision and poetic mind.

The Concept of Design Elements

Design elements are our conceptual tools for visual arts that we will refresh our connection with.

Dots

Each dot is an accomplishment. It is accomplishment of an intention making a point either with the tip of a pencil or by concentrating thoughts and actions.

As unimportant and minimal as they seem, dots are the essential part of any projects. Lines and forms are all offspring of dots and they all can translate back into dots.

Wherever dots are placed, is influenced by their presence. Bring small pieces of blank paper all in the same size and then put a dot in the center of one of them. Then put one dot on the right lower corner of another piece of paper. Next, put a dot even closer to the border of another piece of paper. And look at each one of them one by one and pay attention to your inner sensation. What do you feel from looking at each one of the separately? I will not interfere with the result of your senses by giving a comment before you practice it, but I love to hear from your experiment someday.

Dots are like essential ticking of a clock. They are like simple acts in the moment, as our daily routines. They form a path in our life and if they are placed in the right place and good order, they will bring a sense and meaning to our life according to our deepest intentions. *Every dot makes the difference that every step of yours make. It takes work, commitment and purpose.*

Lines

Lines are continuums of dots. They are in fact dots that are connected to other dots by mediation of some other dots!

A dot in essence can not be stretched to make a line like when we stretch the tip of the pencil on the paper to make a line. What we make on the paper has a micro volume of carbon or paint therefore is three-dimensional. What we talk about (dots, lines) is a two-dimensional virtuality and can only exist in our perception of the world, not in reality. (The two dimensional realm is as virtual as an image in the mirror and products of the processor on a computer screen, possibly showing the truth of tangible realities through non-tangible images.)

The direction in which the dots continue to join, in the given space, and the power of the conviction in the line they form, are what make the line alive.

This conviction is generated by your pure intentions, and strong reasoning for the fact that you are fine the way you are. Are you convinced that you are fine when you are on track of your inner callings?

The strength you create in aligning your spine is conveyed to the line you draw.

Have you noticed how your handwriting changes along with your mood changes?

When you feel fear and lack of confidence, your handwriting is different from when you are feeling content and assured, heading up high with straightened back.

An important drawing practice that benefits both ways is to straighten up your spine and draw long horizontal or vertical lines on a large paper. The good posture makes your lines more powerful and yourself, more confident. Try it and see for yourself.

Now is there any joy or confidence achieved by doing art, using a ruler to draw a line?

Practice drawing long lines on a newspaper or large pieces of paper by coordinating your hand movement and your breath, until you have as much control on your lines as you have on your breathing. Practice till both your hand and your breath dance to the rhyme of your heartbeat. It all happens internally and you will only feel you reached the point by noticing you are relieved, you are delighted.

Shapes

Dots were accomplishments. Continuum of dots formed lines. Now the change in direction of this continuation, can lead to forming shapes, which in turn forms rhythms, meanings and stories.

Shapes are those lines that change their direction and find the way back to themselves. *When the line meets itself, it has formed a shape.* At each turning point some energy from the direction of the line extends and spreads into the space around it.

Imagine a line that is moving toward right side of the paper.

As if it has a momentum, its energy continues to extend a bit further on the paper on the point that it changes direction.

Imagine the tip of a triangle. The space around it seems influenced with this energy. That's how in painting we tend to not place the tips closely facing the borders of the canvas. The energy felt on the tip of an angle is even more when it's acute than when it's wide. You can examine it by moving some cutout triangle shapes around on a blank paper and get a feeling of it.

When the line changes direction continuously, it can form a circle where the energy is very much soft and dispersed evenly.

Now look at an oval shape. Still there are sides of the stretched circle that have more change in direction and influence the space around them softly.

Tone

When drawing, the thickness or fineness of the lines, the number of lines placed close to each other, or the density of lines, the value of the colors that tell the story throughout your piece, creates the tone of your work.

Texture

It is a sense in the lines, or a group of them that calls for a memory of touch, the softness, or roughness. Texture can be created in one line, or by the help of many lines, or many little shapes. Since the actual drawing or painting happens in 3D world, then there is also an actual texture that belongs to the medium you use. The manner you put the paint, how thick or thin, can create an actual texture on the surface of the work that is not an illusion of texture.

Color

We assume colors talk to human only. So we focus on their language, try to understand the words and even derive codes and make signs from them. We forget and remain unaware of the conversation between the colors themselves, and that their language is beyond pieces and words, nothing like codes and signs. And we miss hearing their conversation in awe. In each color exists a world to be explored.
Their realm is where you can study color composition, experience the kindness or roughness of conversation between colors and create a choir or chaos from their voice.

Colors are not like human, but they have a personality! The

origin of all colors is light. They are found in a light form in a spectrum.

Colors in their original light form do not have weight, shape or surface. With a closer look at the linear light spectrum, we will see many areas of color but none of them has a borderline, for example where yellow ends, and green starts.

We assign colors a border on the color wheel to better symbolize each area.

In paintings, we use colors in form of a paste or liquid body that has weight, texture and surface, shapes and size.

Since colors in their nature are components of diffused sunlight, true colors are transparent and reflective in their nature like their source light. True colors have visual qualities like *Chroma,* which is their persona and character, and *Brightness* that is not related to the amount of light received in their essence. In the light spectrum, yellow light seems brighter than green and purple light, even though all of them originate from the same source and amount of light.

Other than Chroma and Brightness, the concept of Color has another quality, which is *Saturation.*

Brightness, symbolize the journey of True colors towards or away from their light source, and Saturation defines their drift towards each other. The three qualities define the location of the color in the virtual color sphere. The concept of color we talk about in visual arts, forms a sphere, which is a virtual reality. It's not tangible but It does exist in the mind.

Imagine a source of light that extends to the extremes of an endless sphere and diffuses into color components in the matrix of the sphere.

The Chroma will be the area and location where the light is born into a family of colors like the red family, or green or purple.

Brightness or the *value* of color shows its location and distance from the source light. The saturation shows the degree of its Chroma in the given color, or purity of its character and energy.

Imagine the Yellow, symbolic color that appears in mind when hear the word yellow. What is the next color to it? Is it perceived Orange? But in fact there are so many colors between them each having a different ratio of yellow and orange in them. Each one is an individual color with the complete list of color qualities. In the area where yellow is located, there is a dimension of the same yellow that goes away from the light source, far deep into shades. This defines the quality of *brightness* or *value* of the color. On the same intense spot of yellow location moving to the opposite direction, pure yellow moves toward lighter shades as it is still pure yellow but lighter and lighter in each move, until it merges with the pure white.

In another direction, the same pure color that we had our attention on can extend and reach bits of other colors from another color area (complementary *colors*). The yellow on a journey towards purple, shows less and less of its personality on each step, it forms a warm brown before the middle of its way until eventually merges with purple.

This explains its *Saturation*, the other quality of color that points at the percentage of a specific chroma (in our case yellow chroma) in a color combination.

What a journey and change a single color goes through and we just see a shell, a sign of it. There is no one-color yellow and no border between yellow and the neighboring colors.

We use pigments to speak of their adventures.

Paints and pigment colors also have the qualities of *Chroma, Brightness* and *Saturation.* The colors we use in tubes or pastel sticks are pigments in a carrier with a reflective quality. Some of them can also mimic the transparency of true colors and the rest are opaque and do not let light pass through them. The opaque colors can cover a layer of painting beneath them. Transparent colors let the under layer show itself. The qualities of color as the medium are not only the *Chroma*, the *Saturation* and the *Brightness* (like in the virtual color world), but also the *opacity.* Opacity also becomes one of our tools. Even though the chemical properties of paints are different, their product is always cooperatively made together.

Color's Statement

Colors in real life are always surrounded by effects of other colors. Therefore in researching each color individually, the color's personality must be studied alone meaning the effects of the surrounding colors, shapes and size must be reduced. You can study colors individually in a background clear from other colors and also a cleared memory from all past mindsets about the color you study. It is as if you ask the color directly how it is like. Though later when you are done with your research, keep in mind that that the colors interact with other visual elements, and their final function is never isolated. So you know when you actually do paintings or design an interior of a home, colors will behave as part of the team around them.

There is always a background to define the colors. At the end it's the feeling or sense of the blue that is perceived as blue in our mind.

Once you try to make a new color with blue and green paint, you will see that 50 percent green and 50 percent blue, makes a color that is hard to pinpoint as the end of green, where blue can start to show up if one percent more blue is added. The perception of colors always depends on the colors of the environment! In an orange-like color surroundings, the 50/50 blue-green will seem more like blue. In a warm red-brownish place it feels more like green. This is due to the physiology of our eyes that always compensates for the colors by a complementary color, to bring a balance. In the orange-like environment, the eyes had already adjusted to orange by sensing more of the complementary color, which is blue. The sense of blue adds to the blue in the actual 50/50 blue-green and the combination feels more like blue. This is a small sample of what happens in the delicate world of color perception in our mind. Imagine orchestrating many colors on a large canvas.

Examine a colored piece of paper, or a tree leaf, in a color-isolated area to see its qualities and how they seem to change in different backgrounds.

Try seeing it on a fully white, completely black, or a neutral gray cardboard.

Then try it on a colored cardboard.

See how the colors never sing alone.

There is no absolute statement for colors in the real world.

It is the time and new conditions that make the statement of the color in our mind not exactly the color itself. What they say varies depending on the rest of the members in the orchestra. Colors do not communicate individually!

The beauty of colors is in their cooperation and teamwork not in their individuality and intensity. They adjust themselves with each other and often yield to each other. The warm brown seems *cool* when it is next to more red browns and it seems *warm* next to the greens. The milder the intensity of their personalities, the more welcoming they are to their adjacent colors. Every shade of color is beautiful and special and has its own place on the color wheel! They communicate as one unit, one composition together with all the other elements like lines, shapes, extent of surface area within the frame of work.

Color-coding

Using colors as codes has been a great way to organize human communications, signs, notes and labels. Using color as a sign organizes sequences of actions to make the massive details of life easier and safe like in traffic.

As it has been helpful, the use of its organizing qualities has expanded to lots of logos and social affairs too!

But we cannot identify a color by its assigned job in our daily life. Just as we cannot identify a person by the position they are assigned at work in the day. The essence of the employee is much greater, finer and more important than the temporary position they have at hand now.

In color-coding and signs, colors are employed to convey meanings regardless of what they themselves have to say. We speak of warning signs as red flags whereas the same red can be in the flower petals and is not sign of danger.

Like any brand logo that may influence our choice, Color-coding has an effect on our choices of colors and true communication with them in visual arts. It often interferes with our relationship to colors during the day as we see things too. Usually when we see a solid color, the mind starts up the coding menu trying to find and to read a massage; a boy or a girl, a yes/a no? Which medical research or cause or political views! Over thinking color-coding interferes with the deep understanding of the colors.

It substitutes a highly designed default sense with a particular human made program in path of mind perception of the colors.

Other than considering colors as signs and codes, there is a psychological aspect of colors and symbolism according to the language of our psyche, which is meant to be a shared and common language. The scientific information about it is usually found in art and psychology texts. Make sure when you read about the psychological meanings of colors in a text, always check your feelings about the color in your imagination first. In other words, meet the color in your imagination before you read about it, so you can find out your own feelings about the color. Allow your senses probe for the impression of the color on your mind. Sense your own way through the knowledge of color theory and psychology of colors as you study the texts about it. There is no point in applying colors into your work only according to an instructional manual, because you, as a part of this triangle of conversation, have a unique position that can change the dialog. This unique position cannot be considered in a manual, and that dialog is the only dialog that should find its way into your paintings.

Don't Take the Medium for the Technique

Oil color is the medium to paint with; Painting with oils is painting with liquid paint, the pigments in an oil carrier/ binder.

Chalk or pastels have those pigments in another binder. But they both have color, the pigments that are used in a painting.

Chalk, pastels, oil paints are tangible mediums. Drawing and painting are the techniques.

When you draw lines with red oil paint to show a geometric summary of an object, it's still a drawing.

When you try to draw in black and white in a way to create an illusion of something, creating patches of color or tones, it's a painting. A painting can be black and white and a drawing can be colorful regardless of their medium.

When you start sketching with oil paints on a canvas, it's a drawing at first. As you proceed to define the shapes and space, tones or colors, your work turns into a painting, whereas the medium did not change.

To Be an Artist

Are spots of oil paint on my jeans and face a sign that I am an artist? How about my colorful canvas? Is any colorful painting, really artistic?

Is the intensity of my colors, a proof that I have powerful knowledge of color?

Or does the variety of the colors in my painting show the abundance of my creativity?

Is painting a symmetrically balanced composition, a proof to my capability of creating balance in my paintings?

Are the flowers and the bowl that stand out of the canvas, a proof of my art or is it just a skill to make a three dimensional illusion?

Is the perfect rendering of muscles, the flesh, the anatomy, a proof of one's artistic abilities? Is knowledge and experience the only indicators of quality in an artwork?

The artist is the one who incorporate all the skills with the now, as configured, compassionate and honest as possible, with no expectation of being approved.

Compassion in art form, is not painting the poor and the hungry, it is not even painting moments of giving or receiving donations and gifts. This gives rise to compassion in the viewers for the subject but does not imply compassion in art. Not the music that weeps with the injured, but the music that soothes the injured is compassionate.

To be an artist, you do not need only to paint, sing or make music ... You need to sense the beauty, to be able to tune into the flow of beauty in your life, in every bit, and to try to keep your balance at each point, in each moment. The balance that mediates between *self-compassion* versus *compassion for others,* until they merge into one.

It is not only the craftsmanship, but the wisdom and love behind it that makes a piece, a work of Art.

Balancing Passion, Compassion and Self-compassion in Art Practice

How can we actualize the balance between Self-compassion and Compassion for others while following our Passion in practicing art?

Self-Compassion in Physical Level:

- Keeping up with a time wise schedule to work so you don't override the rhythms of your body like sleep and rest at night.
- Using materials and working with mediums that are non-toxic, with no hazard to your health.

For example it doesn't matter that technically, first layer of oil painting must be diluted by thinners to dry faster. If thinners were toxic and a hazard to my health or others, I would put them aside and think of another method of drying, or work my way around it letting go of layer painting!

- Keeping the environment, the air where you work clean as you breath in the materials in it. If avoiding the toxicity were not possible then using ventilation would be next option.
- Keeping a good posture during work, so your body will not suffer during the time you put your full attention on art.

Self-Compassion in Emotional and Mental Level:

- Now this painting is the kingdom of your subconscious mind. You must not let self-blame, all patterns of thoughts that judge and condemn your drawing, drive you while you do art. Put them all on pause.
- Painting with no self-abuse, which is working with a sense of extracting profit or any benefit from your joyful practice. This should be on pause too!

Here where we are doing art, is the realm of seeking; we don't know what we end up with, especially if we have just started to dig up the layers of our thoughts and emotions.

Have a sense of openness and understanding that the inner dialog comes from the immediate level of the subconscious mind, where all pain and hurt and questions are stored. Soon as we are open and forgiving to ourselves, this level releases its contents, which may well show up in our painting. If as a result, the paintings that are done have a negative effect on you, you can keep the artwork separately or even wipe it off.

So being patient, and being a non-judgmental and kind listener as we hear the background dialog of our mind, is a key.

Compassion for others in Physical level:

- **Respecting** other peoples' space and comfort while you work. For example work in a designated area, or if the space is shared with others, make sure they are ok with it.
- **Maintaining** the purity of air as it belongs to everyone who breathes it in. So using air ventilation takes the toxins away from work space to the atmosphere may not be

enough for this purpose and it's better to work in a way that requires less or no use of toxic materials.
- **Using environmental friendly materials** if possible, or adjust your work and make it more simple.
- **Recycling** paper and carefully recycling possible toxic materials.
- **Reusing** containers before recycling them.

Compassion for Others in Emotional Levels:

The manifestation of compassion in Art simply is to heal and not to hurt. Having kind intentions will lead your work to a compassionate level regardless of the subject of your work.

After listening to your self talks with no judgment and practicing to embrace your feelings, you have been kind enough to yourself to allow best intentions develop in your mind, and they will flow into your work and to others from there. Your work will inherently have emotional benefits to your viewers as well.

Tooo Much Skill

Sometimes skills you have acquired, create a frame around what you do which is so strong that your mind feels quite content and secure, and gives up exploration, forgets its artistic freedom and never-ending discoveries. You may find yourself mastering what you have already mastered. Once you remember the never-ending possibilities to grow, you are to challenge the frame of habits and styles in order to set yourself free.

This frame of habit is about the perfect connection made between the mind, brain and body in performing your art. You have created the perfect connection by practicing flawlessly and long enough to improve mind-hand coordination in a specific way, which easily relays your intentions to your hands to perform. This is a station to rest and enjoy after years of hard work. But don't forget the big picture; that those intentions are fluid, and the artist's mind needs an outlet to freely travel not only in these roads but also beyond them. And now that a strong habit is stabilized, with no flexibility for an outlet, your mind rests in it for a while doing effortless and joyful work. After the rest when it's time to explore, it is trapped in its own fabric. Routes to what was wanted once act as barriers now. You can form any style of doing art into skilled craftsmanship, but you should also practice moving beyond the skills, once in a while.

Remember as you develop your craftsmanship and your style, also master in your supervision over the big picture of the paths and habits you are making. Change those habits every now and then, do it a new way. Nothing is the end of it; there is always room for expansion by exploring more possibilities.

Summary

- Focus on your body rhythms as you do art. Don't compromise sleep. Be physically active. Have exercise become an essential part of your art practice.
- Avoid toxins and erosive habits that can build up as you do art ... Pay attention to your posture. Take a break every once in a while and move for few minutes. You'll be able to reduce future effects of long hours of sitting and better tune in to your best quality of thinking.
- As you do art, listen to your inner self, rather than listening to your immediate mind commands.

- Know that in the beginning your mind cleanses itself, so at first you'll hear inner demands that are not truly *yours*. Ignore them and keep on practicing a new way.
- You will pass this level and gradually you'll hear and feel your inner urges. Be gentle and don't ignore them, embrace them. Do the art the way your heart wants. Your heart cannot harm you or others.

Here you are deeply connected with subconscious mind.
You will find insight and a vision of your truth.
Where your truth is, you can't find anything but beauty.
This is the gift of art to you.
Now you are a gifted artist.

Talent is not the gift. You earn talent by passionately practicing what you love.
What a world it would be if it were filled with gifted artists who were given the vision of beauty.
Their works of art will be the gift of happiness to the world.
If Art can heal hearts, revive hope and do good for the world, it does it through You the Artist.

Chapter V

Art & Children

"I can see clearly today this entire universe is on purpose. I see now that our earliest personality traits and predilections are expressed because they represent our highest selves. At these early ages we are still very much connected to our Source, because we haven't yet had the chance to ***e****dge* ***G****od* ***o****ut and assume the mantle of the false self, which is the ego."*

— Dr. Wayne W. Dyer

From "I Can See Clearly Now", Chapter 1

Art & Children

Art is a path to self-discovery for adults. It leads to the place of the eternal self. Children though, have just come from there. They have recently come to this new state, encountering the world of being. They have not yet been much far from their eternal self. They are still tuned with their source, and they need a venue to express all the joy and the emotional values of meeting this new world. In this world everything is excitingly new, even a breeze.

Children, like adults, get emotional, sense the unknown that is the fear, and experience stress and anxiety as much as their plate can take. But in terms of expressing the anxiety and stress, not only don't they identify their feelings; whether it is sadness, anger or fear, but also they don't have a good supply of words to express the feelings.

They know well how to fix it though! They know how to let it go if we grown ups remotely support and supervise them rather than interfere directly with their natural ways of eliminating the fear and anxiety. Children would play, would sing their spontaneous songs, they would mourn the loss of a toy, and they will draw their own lines and find relief.

As soon as they develop the ability to put a mark on a surface at a young age, they will do it whether by food or by their finger and the sand. They express it all in the most perfect and unique way. *Art is meant to be one of many ways of expression for children especially when they are under school age.*

Art for kids is all about expression. No one knows if their song was in wrong notes or pitch, because the notes, and the silence in between were exactly adjusted to their deep emotions that were supposed to be expressed, released and let go. So are their drawings and paintings.

Art Instruction for Children

Young children tune with both the physical world and the inner world simultaneously. This will spark bursts of energy and excitement in them showing up as jumping, shouting, laughing, and crying which are all forms of expression! Art instruction for children builds around this fact and adapts to the age and demands of the child who is doing art.

At very young age, they only need remote supervision and guidance about use of art tools and safety. We may not know if their paintings should be accompanied with a certain personal dance, and which melody should they sing along with the dance, or if they should just sit in one place and silently and deeply concentrate while painting. But children themselves do know it. They know if it's time to express or if it's time to observe or research the world around them. There is no format they should fit their colors in, no cartoon or 2D model that they should try to reproduce at this age. Have you ever seen how some children feel stressed, feel so hot as they challenge themselves to draw from an assigned art pattern?

When they are guided through this way, they are moving away from seeing the beauty and their own way of expression of it. Instead they will have to align themselves with the expressions of adult artists, an alignment that gives them frustration.

Trying to align themselves with assigned shapes makes the children feel that their ways of art expression are not valid, their idea is not valid, and their emotions are not important. So children conclude that probably they are not valid.

They will then look for approval by trying to perfectly copy someone else's design (Same thing happens for adults who follow the popular trends for approval). Now that's how the children are stressed and feel overheated; these are beginning steps to forget the fact that one's innate values are always approved. Children want to make sure that they are accepted, their performance and capabilities are valid and eventually they are valuable beings. If they can't assure themselves through the approval of their adult caregivers, they lose the self-respect which they are born with. This is a starting point to gradually lose self compassion as well.

Teaching them techniques to draw one circle for an apple, several circles for a flower, could question their ability of evaluation and research. It also convinces them that there is only one solution, only one way to see and one way to draw things as if there is a secret that they have to know in order to draw correctly.

Children under age seven mostly communicate nonverbally. They understand, learn, and love above words, through actions and relations. Non-verbal messages given to children when they do art must be fully considered. The nonverbal message given above in art practice, does not match the reality about drawing and painting. They may buy into the wrong message: that they really don't know how to do it themselves, so they need to follow the patterns.

Following instruction to use human made appliances and tools like new cars, a new cell phone and so on, is necessary. Art, though is not human made. It is human's inheritance. Art techniques are derived from this inherited source. So everybody has access to art creativity as much as they need to. Beauty is everywhere and human no matter how young, is the lover of beauty. In the absence of beauty and balance in life, children feel more pressured than adults, on the other hand they have less ways to express it than adults, so it is their definite right to use authentic art coming from their source to express and set themselves free, by drawing, singing or playing.

Children's art is the natural manifestation of the creative

power they have inherited for their growth. *Art is simply the child's way of Being.*

Support and Supervision

Instead of instructing young children how to draw, we can support them on their way of making art by our knowledge of how to protect the artist within the child. Also our other important role is our awareness of their environment, materials and the risk factors and safety tips.

Art making should only be remotely supervised for children under nine. Have the place safe and comfortable; provide non-toxic material, non-harmful objects. Create a loving and embracing atmosphere to welcome the beauty of diversity in their creative work. Before the session starts, nurture yourself, with good rest and deep breathing to welcome the joy of creativity in you first. If you are running an art practice session for groups, set kind limits of behavior and rules for children so they nonverbally learn the value of kindness as they do art. They learn how to treat each other nicely, as you teach them to be kind to and considerate of each other. Learning the value of kindness in an art session is necessary because it relates to the great arts of living in future. Yet about doing the Art, they are the ones to decide if it's time to paint or to just doodle on paper.

They should not be encouraged to color within the line unless they want to do so. Nor should they be encouraged to splash paint and apply all colors, if they don't feel like it. They know better.

Instructions on color combination formulas, like a formula for what color does red make when mixed with yellow, are not useful before they experiment it themselves. Memorizing formulas just fills in a load in their mind, which is not truly functional. Instead ask them how does red talk to you? Provide them with a question that guides their attention to the subject and allows them find the answer from their personal point of view. This redirects them to tune in their heart language; their sensory language. From there they can recognize the color's personality and characteristics holistically by the heart. In last chapter we worked hard on undoing our color-coded mindsets, to be able to connect with true impression of colors. Children have much shorter way to the goal if they are led to this direction.

Ask them how does red talk to orange? There is no dividing line between them. So they may feel the two are close friends.

Encourage them to listen to the colors, instead of instructions. Ask them what do you hear from color red and color blue? Maybe they want to reach out and hold hands and when they do, their hands seem like another color. The name of the color is not as important as their experiment of mixing them and seeing the new color. There is no art formula to be taught, this is the calling of a new purple to be heard.

To do authentic art, young kids need instruction-free support and supervision. Children don't really need any direct or indirect art instruction before age nine or ten, or until they call for it from their heart. Even then, still the instruction must be according to their demand.

Children Research Physical Qualities!

Kids have a tendency for research in an authentic scientific method. Soon as they have a grip control, they will check the new item they see by its sound. They hit it to table, hit things together and if they are stuck in a high dining chair they will throw it, so they will hear its sound when it hits the ground! It is the same with other senses of taste and touch. They test physical properties like tensile qualities, viscosity, weight and finally the heat to an extreme of sacrifice! Those extremes are where they really need to be supervised and protected, not in every little, harmless experiment.

As they grow up, they want to put these physical realities on paper, or in clay. They do the same with their feelings and inner realities and put them together on paper, like when they miss someone, they try to draw that person. Instructing art techniques too early in life without supporting their feelings, personal expressions and experiments leads them to a misunderstanding of both their own feelings and art.

Not every skillful technique will host the spirit of art in itself, nor does art need that much fuss around it. Skill full art techniques and craftsmanship are not the art itself, but are the vessels to host it. Authenticity of the content is the art.

If we encourage little kids to copy illustrations and follow rules in drawing, then how can we expect them to be creative and authentic at work or in their life as adults in future?

Eventually not all kids want to become a visual artist when they grow up, even though they all like to paint and draw and research. If they want to practice a form of art professionally though, they really need a free format and secure feelings about self-expression and research, from the very beginning of doing art in their early years.

This is a personal decision and even parents cannot know if choosing a path for them to become professional artist in future will really work, before the children know about their inner callings. The children need freedom to decide whether they want to be a professional artist themselves or, it will not be art what they will do on a mandatory practice. The wisdom of their inner master will carry them through and we as parents and teachers should trust this wisdom.

Offer them freedom and support on their way. They need to have the ownership of their sacred language, whether they want to become an artist or not.

Emotional Cleansing in Children

Doing art in form of painting / music like percussion, and forming clay along with sports like running and etc. are harmless ways to express the emotions in children. If the emotions are not expressed, they may shake inside and eventually harm somebody and that somebody is usually the child who holds it in. By the way, consider the vocabulary of a six-year-old and that of an adult. The child has very limited vocabulary and also less experience and skill for reasoning and convincing others about his or her boundaries.

The children certainly need a nonverbal outlet to empty and cleanse their reservoir of emotions and thoughts. For this reason, they must feel assured that they are not blamed or made fun of, for doing art their own way. Neither should they be encouraged to copy arts of other artists.

Children around six must have access to a very intimate language for communication with their inner world and the world outside. This is an anchor that keeps them centered when daily life brings them confusion. Visual language is the quiet and personal form of communication that feels safe to the child. They trust this way of communication and they must have access to a simple and intact relationship with themselves while doing art. They must not be criticized, directed, instructed or led to copy any image in visual art or they may lose track of what they are able to do.

Allow them space and time to communicate with inner presence to resolve their confusions though the motion of their hands. This is not only a communicating with their own intellect but also a release of tension from the body. That is why percussion music feels liberating. So is an informal dance. If they are drawing, they might combine the drawing with a dance or percussion, or just a free drawing that perforates the paper!

Sometimes the children press the tip of their pen too hard on the paper, and make holes in it, and this will do the job for them to de-stress! They must be releasing the tension stored in their arm, which usually comes from anger, from something that seemed unfair to them but they could not pin point and express it, or maybe they couldn't allow themselves to confess the anger to their selves. They can grow out of that emotion sooner once they release it to the paper. After all they are evolving souls that are led through their path naturally.

Of course sometimes they will not be happy with the results of their drawings because when they have something to release, the drawing can actually turn into a mess. They come to the adult supervisor, complain and cry about it. Well, it's better to listen to them rather than looking at what they think is a mess, finding the flaw and teaching them how to do it and how to prevent it. This drama is part of a bigger story. Nothing has been wrong with the painting. Be a listener to them and an admirer of their courage. Take it easy. Suggest them a break, so that they can drink some water and cool down, and whenever they are ready they can start all over again if they want. There may be some other complex emotions showing up each time in their painting and I wish I could point out at each one of the cases, because every case is so different that can't be put all into only a couple of suggestions. But I'm sure if you nurture yourself before the session and if you practice the art as a path to your self-discovery, you can trust the wisdom that will support your responses in unexpected situations at class.

I am sure that even most kindly instructed drawing methods using templates and patterns and formats to children, blocks some of the outlets of expression and builds up some tension.

Bringing home those template drawings and receiving some admiration, does no good, because it turns the mind constructive aspect of art, into a paper constructive art. On the other hand, too many *dos* and *don'ts* about their drawing at class, gives them a hard time and they give up. This is why some kids dislike drawing.

Some other kids pass this time of life, with their expressive tools and outlets intact and they retain their good relationship with their ways of expression in art for long. As they grow up over the age of six, they must have released lots of childhood confusions about their young life experience.

Art Lessons for Kids as They Grow Older

It is a great brain exercise for children over nine, or whenever they are ready, to explore perception of the spatial world they live in, within the language of the eyes.

We know that the spatial world is three dimensional, but the image of it in our eyes is two dimensional. Our brain translates it back to three dimension to have correct understanding of the space.

Actively translating the perceived third dimension, again to two dimensional language of the eyes, is a wonderful mind exercise that happens in life drawing. Teachers would never want to put already made 2D patterns or pictures in front of a child to draw from if they know it deprives the student from chance of developing this power. If children are given the opportunity to explore a bowl of fruits and then draw based on imagination, you will see how different these paintings are, not only based on their ability to draw, but based on the variety of their authentic personal view points; physical location or emotional location that day!

It will be helpful (if they like it) to offer the older children exploring a three dimensional object like a single fresh orange or apple, a vase, and suggesting them to touch and evaluate it, then draw what they see after their tactile experience. This adds to the depth of their understanding about the object, and an active translation of the 3D perception to a 2D image will be easier for them later. This practice invites them to future art lessons for drawing from realities, a style called *realism*.

Art for kids over nine years old must lead to an open door to investigate the world, not to the ready-made designs, templates and repetition thereafter. It is the kids choice which area to focus on. As they grow up, if they are satisfied with enough expressive art work through their childhood, in anytime they might be interested to practice drawing more precisely and realistically, where academic art instruction can gradually kick in their art experience.

Often I hear about kids with higher IQs, who can precisely copy the cartoon images or illustrations they were given to draw from, and are admired for their work. Of course they can do it, but they can do much better and more as well. Reproduction of pictures and patterns is not the language of expression and will not favor their IQ either. Are they being deprived of developing their emotional language because they are very smart and can please the eyes by reproducing images very well?

They will love to do art for a few more years of triumph in receiving the admiration of grownups and once they notice the message that they are giving to themselves by copying, they may quit doing art.

They should have had this sacred form of expression open. A safe and secure environment with freedom to express the wanted, and expel the unwanted, is what's needed for all children including very smart kids.

Erasers

Suggesting kids to have an eraser at hand when they draw, means to them; "there is an ideal pattern and you may not be able to make it easily. You may fall short of doing it properly so you must redo it several times and you must hide the footprints of the mistakes because they are the signs of lack of ability. Therefore bring an eraser with you when you come to class!"

That's why erasers are not welcome in my classes. But the students with all their right or wrong ways of drawing are welcomed. Because every mistake they make, points at a door to a specific mind body exercise to be designed for them while practicing art.

There is no mistake that cannot be compensated by another correct line. All of those mistakes are forgivable and once you notice them, they become a platform for progress! If there is no way to fix a drawing by correct lines, then there is always a new blank paper to embrace their new painting. This is how they can learn the art of living.

Yes, also paper should be used responsibly, then reused and then recycled.

Art History for Children

Art history is a wonderful source of learning about the journey and transformation of the face of art during centuries. Not that art has ever evolved; art has always been perfect from the time cavemen painted on the walls of the caves. Art transformation has been a reflection of the change in the mind of the society within centuries. In some periods, human had been in the awe of nature and realism, some periods reflected human in awe of divinity, and some in the impression of nature on individual human minds. History of art is great source of knowledge to everyone, but for kids it is more about hearing *the story of art*, rather than *history* of it, unless they show interest to learn it as an assignment. Children must retain their sacred ways of expression for many years.

Childhood is still the time for kids to run on their own soul's philosophy and purpose that's unknown to us.

Sometimes the work and life of few famous visual artists in art history, is chosen to be taught to young children. Hearing their life story, and seeing their art masterpieces is a great source of inspiration for children. The manner and style of these great artists though, are too complicated to be summarized in a session, and to be taught to kids as a style of painting.

The brush strokes, and the style the artist had developed in years of hard work. Even if the lesson is well learned, it is not clear if it would benefit the kids at all? It shows that they could do it, but also proves their own expressive art abilities wrong. If they really manage to perfectly copy the style of the great artist, they have actually taken a step away from their own authentic art. If the children ever believe this is art, they have taken an illusion of art for true art.

After all, none of those famous artists in the art history that are chosen as role models for children's art, developed their art skills this way in their childhood.

Children are already in great relationship and placement with the core of visual art, vocal music and theatrical art at its beginning levels. There would always be time to learn techniques later.

Having to copy a great artist's work is nothing but either giving them a feeling that they are less than enough, or taking them to a least creative path, copying, that even though there is no end to it, never satisfies a personal sense of achievement.

Teaching children art history by taking them to art museums and galleries, or showing them pictures of great paintings in the history of art, reading them books and telling them stories about art and biography of artists, will provide them the right connection and inspiration.

They will enjoy visiting museums and get an idea where paintings can end up to! The joy of a field trip to museum, and the hope they find, by seeing how their paintings can be valued, is the best thing art history can teach them.

Trends of Our Days

Children are exposed to a lot of sound effects and the visual complexes that don't contain the loving spirit of art. Images that show only half a second and are followed by the next image which disappears quickly again. The camera views that move so fast to the left or right, that you must run eyes to follow them. The background pictures that change or move towards you or away from you constantly.

Repetitive rhythms and sudden changes that create harsh sounds in music or visual distress in computer arts, are unfavorable experiences for the mind. We must have overridden our natural reactions, to be able to live our daily life today, hearing the radio, TV, watching movies in theatre or playing electronic games that use these techniques.

They all create visual or auditory shocks that are not used deliberately. It may seem all right, because it is the trend of the day. But the effects of it may not be known yet.

Giving constant visual shocks overrides the choice of attention. It attracts attention by force; It brings one to watch something by compelling the eye and ears. Adults may leave their seat, if they are not used to it already, but children may sit and watch it to the end.

In a better way, drawing attention could have been also possible by reasoning, or by pointing at relation of the subject of art to common sense, which everyone has access to.

But for now what should you do for your child, your niece, your students? The trends may have a place in life routines, and it's no good to suddenly reject them all.

You can start minimizing the negative effects by doing simple things.

Take Children for a Walk Outside

To teach art to your kids, take them out for a walk, in nature. Nature is not far but right by your door. Instead of usual habits of rush, plan to have a ten minute walk dedicated to new discoveries. You and your child together, listen to the sounds of birds, find them on the trees. You may have to extract the sound of birds chirping, from between the harsh sounds of leaf blowers or drillings. If it happens often then it's even more heartwarming to know that the birds are still singing there at the same time. And you had been able to drive your senses to a very fine tuned level to hear them!

Look together for any sprouts on the ground or any flower buds. Discover the tiniest insects on the ground where you walk together. This brings their senses back to their fine level, which was eroded by the harsh sound and visual effects.

The ten-minute walk approves your child's delicate inner values, and develops his or her sense of seeing beauty, knowing that the beauty shines as strongly always and everywhere. This connection with beauty is the main block children need, in order to build their artistic experiences.

Chapter VI

Beauty in You

The Beauty in You

From seeing beauty in the world, a path is paved to see the inherent beauty in you.

A lie will never register in *you*, even if you tell it to yourself.

Your eternal presence is made from such truth, love, and beauty that can't allow a lie to enter its fields. The lie would feel like pain inside even if it worked to your benefit. There is an innocent, loving nature in you which wants to resonate with boundless beauty and truth. The slightest lie feels like pain even if it is only considering yourself inferior or unlovable. Feeling inferior and unlovable does not resonate with your truth, therefore it is like a lie that makes you feel bad in your skin. It stops the inner beauty from shining out. The beauty becomes imprisoned inside you until the day you notice this self-talk is not true and you change it.

We cannot do much to change our outer appearance as our beauty. The way we appear in this world gives us no clue to our inner beauty. Our options for seeing inner beauty are in what we do, what we create, and how harmonious it is with our definite inner beauty. When the waves of what we do and how we think resonate with our inner truth rather than interfere, we become clear and our inner beauty can be seen. The beauty inside is in everyone. It is bound with love and rooted in truth. Therefore it can emanate from inside out when the entire path is clear. It is the state of clarity that brings peace to you, the honesty with yourself that allows your inner beauty to shine out.

Being Yourself is Authentic and the Most Beautiful Way to Be

The most honest way to be is to be yourself.

The most beautiful way to be is to be yourself.

The easiest way to be is also to be yourself.

When you are yourself, you are authentic.

So being authentic is the easiest way to be!

It is much harder of a struggle trying not to be *you*!

Trying to be like someone else consumes so much energy that it lowers your ability to remain calm. If you decided to do so, the slightest criticism can burst you to extreme anger, internally or externally.

Celebrate who you are by simply being the way you truly are, for there is no other truthful and beautiful way to be.

Walking the Way to Yourself

It requires courage to walk the way to know one's true self, the true and beautiful self.

If you think there is not a happy ending in seeing yourself at the end, know that this is an idea you bought into at a young age.

You would never buy it if it were offered to you now. Take another look and examine this idea.

There is a jewel in you.

There is something precious in your existence. Just remove the shells away and you'll see it.

Michelangelo was asked how he managed to make the magnificent sculpture of David. He replied that he did not make it. He saw the David in the stone; he removed the excess stone and released the angel.

Michelangelo must have felt the presence of David by inner

vision, carefully hammering on the exact parts of the stone, carving out gently, layer by layer not to hurt David's figure, until David appeared out of marble in his complete form.

This may be the story of humans seeking their eternal truth. Navigating through life, with no proof, but an inner conviction.

But the conviction is not enough; actions are needed, making points, and creating rhythms tenderly and carefully. We work on and on, until what we long dreamed of finally appears. The world can be filled with this kind of work when we all appear out of our illusions and confusions.

Start practicing to see beauty as soon as possible. Follow the thread from the outer beauty of the sky and nature to the far ends of eternity, where you discover your true self. At the end, who you become is who you have always been.

You are not new to the universe, you were always known.

But this new *you* is a new self-image that better represents your truth.

A self-image that cannot change by resolution alone but by thousands of small and important actions, like the dots that compose the shape of your drawing.

Being your true self is as dynamic as beauty is. Once you reach the state of being yourself, it is still not the end.

The waves under the surf board never stop, and you will keep on balancing yourself by changing gestures, only this time confidently and more easily. Even when you seem still, your mind needs to continuously adapt to the new flow of life events. Being *your* true self is a state of meditation in motion.

How Long Does It Take to Get There?

If you get an electrocardiogram when your heart is beating fast, to monitor and record your heartbeat on paper, it takes a long strip of paper from the fast heart rates to where they reach a normal rate. It may have taken such long distance on paper for your heart to calm down. But your calm heart has been in the same place from the time the beats were fast, until now that they have calmed down. That is how long it feels from when you search for your truth until you get there. But your true self is with you all the time.

You may take on a long journey on land to find yourself, only to know at the end that *you* have always been there. All along, the destination was under your feet! You just had to walk enough steps to realize it!

The entire path, as far as it can be, has been taken in one place, right there, in your heart.

You have always been there; you just had to walk enough till you find the strength and awareness to feel calm...and to feel your presence. This is why it's important not to rush, to take your time, to rest after each step.

Your heart rests after each beat, and never stops doing this during your life. This is the secret of the hardest working muscle in the body; rest in turn for each work.

The best way to beat is to beat within rhythms, like the heart. The rhythm of *letting go* of a contraction, and gaining it back, is what provides the continuum of life. The heart lets go of the contraction for life flow. *Follow your heart* on your way.

Hard work doesn't need to become a hard time. Do not learn it the hard way.

Keep doing what you do, but rest meanwhile. You act and you rest. Then act and rest. And this is a new story that goes on. *It is the silence of rest between the actions you take that accomplishes your work, not the constants repetition of the action or rest.*

Live on and thrive through hard work with joy, satisfaction and rest. Permission is not needed.

Endnote

This is what I know about *art*; it doesn't have to be fancy, trendy, or entertaining. It doesn't need to be like something, and doesn't need to be *liked* by anyone.

It just needs to be an honest work, non-judgmental and receptive of the truth. Free from artificial gestures, but full of love. Art is what inspires you and others. Art itself has no need to be promoted in our societies. *Art is in fact supposed to promote us and our societies.* There is no use in practicing art, or speaking of art without having it manifest in your thinking and life style.

Art making is like examining a model path to handle actual life situations, and *not to* miss out on living by falling into repetitive thinking and actions, but sensing the world without a pre-made mindset, with no rush, and with no hesitation or doubt.

It's an instruction of how to go on, if not how to stop, and to be patient with your impatience when you feel lost.

Believe it or not, *art* takes exactly the shape of your inner, your personal inner world, the one that only you know of, or it is not *art.*

Art is the gift to anyone who traveled to this world of being. It is not just for the most talented, or the most privileged, but for everyone. The most talented mastered it because they attended to it, loved it and practiced it more.

There is no mistake on the road and there is always a chance to redo and renew. This road has a place where you can rest and nest for a while; but remember to leave tomorrow when it's time to explore again. There is a lot to find on the way, in wonder, in admiration.

And the best souvenir you bring back with you is not what you found on your path, or what you made from it. It is who you became after the journey. You transformed your shells to become translucent and let the real you shine through. The real you that you thought you had lost.

Now you can do a lot. Now you know. Now you are who you truly are. You know the way, you know the beauty, you tasted pure love, and now the routes of disappointment are only short round trips that you'll never get stuck in again. You can bring insight to the other commuters by just being the way you are, honest, loving, content and assured.

Art can clear your way to find out what is all this fuss about in life, and to become surprised at the end of the road to find out that the answer has always been right by you.

Find a view on art that brings wisdom, not only knowledge of Art history and techniques.

Become more peaceful internally and spread the seeds of peace everywhere. That is possible only when you see the glory in yourself, the jewel inside that has been covered in layers of shells, the true inner beauty that's for you and for the world to see.

Get closer to your *true self* through *art*, practice art consciously and responsibly with good intention and it eventually guides you through creating your ultimate masterpiece.

At the end, if you do not feel like doing art at all, just set practicing art aside, and simply practice being yourself. Put anything you learned and liked in this book about art into the ways you manage your life, and be artistically *your true self.* That is by far a great art.

P.S. And don't forget to gaze at the sky, a tree or a small potted plant for a minute every day.

Printed in the United States
By Bookmasters